This Book Belongs To

____

がんばって ください！

By: **Oil Painting Lovers Publishing**

Hiragana Writing Practice Sheet 1

か (ka) き (ki) く (ku) け (ke) こ (ko)

Hiragana Writing Practice Sheet 3

さ (sa) し (shi) す (su) せ (se) そ (so)

Hiragana Writing Practice Sheet 4

た (ta) ち (chi) つ (tsu) て (te) と (to)

な (na) に (ni) ぬ (nu) ね (ne) の (no)

は (ha) ひ (hi) ふ (fu) へ (he) ほ (ho)

や (ya) ゆ (yu) よ (yo)

ら

り

る

れ

ろ

Hiragana Writing Practice Sheet 10

わ (wa) を (o) ん (n)

Writing Practice Sheet

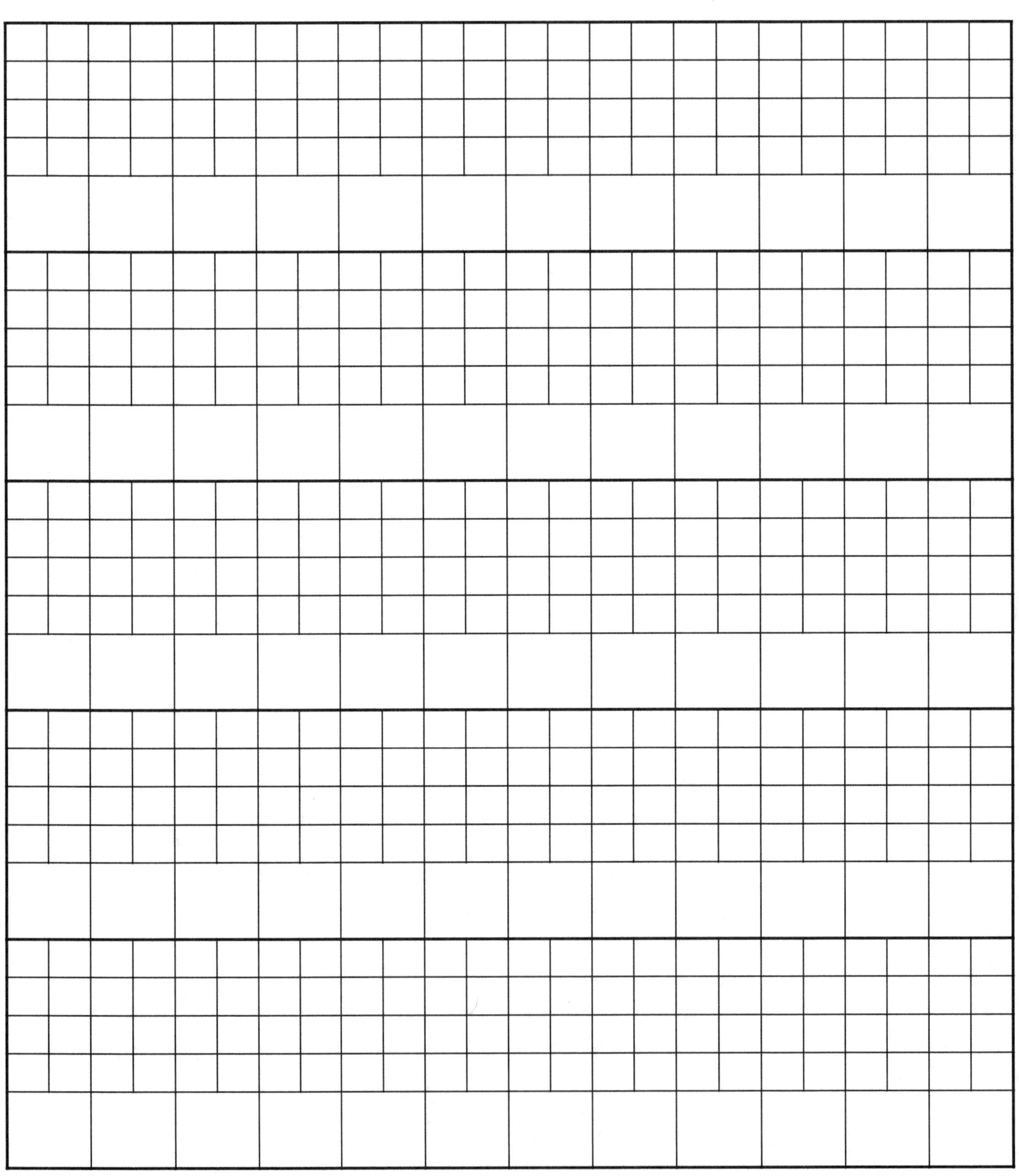

Writing Practice Sheet

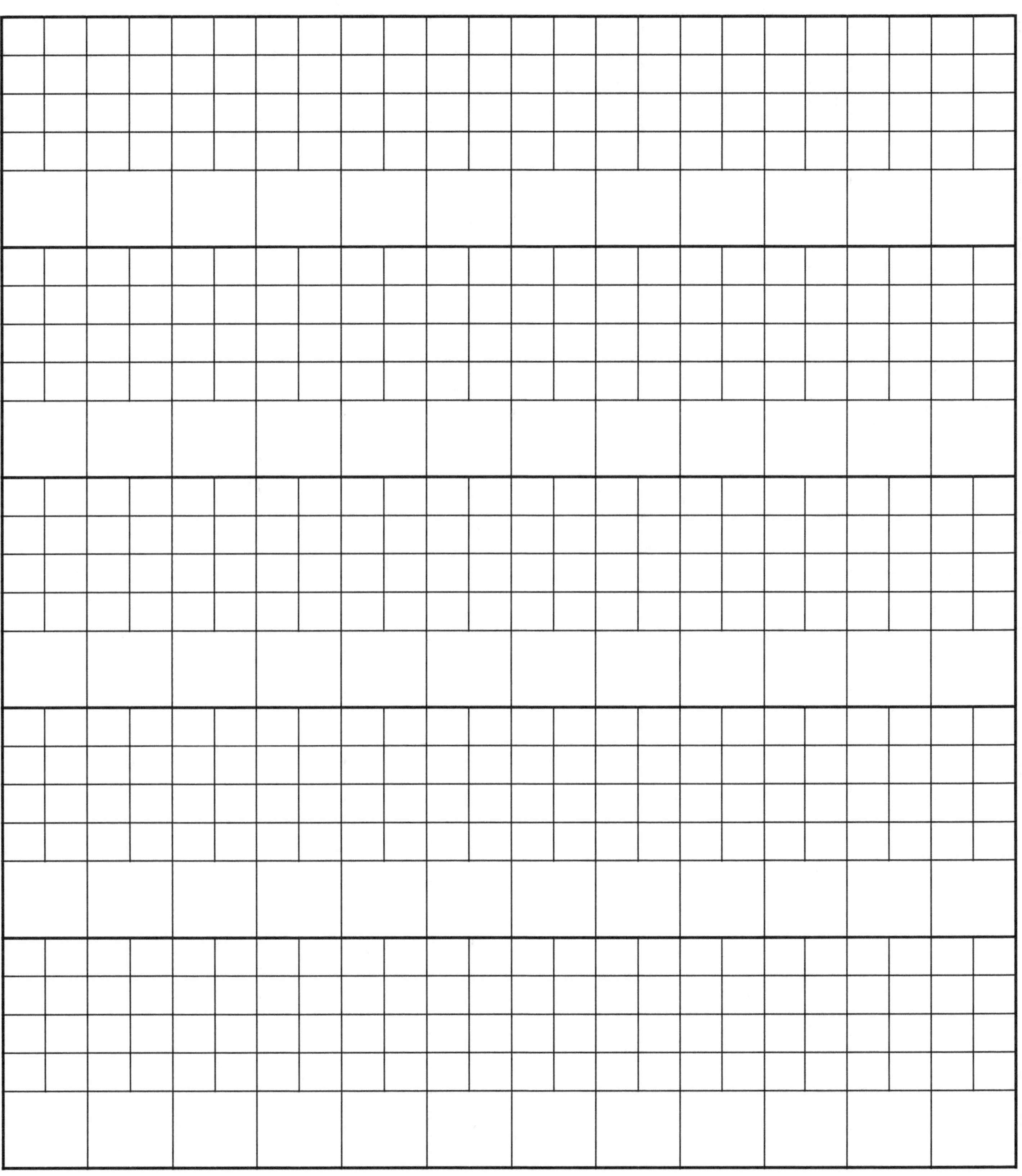

Writing Practice Sheet

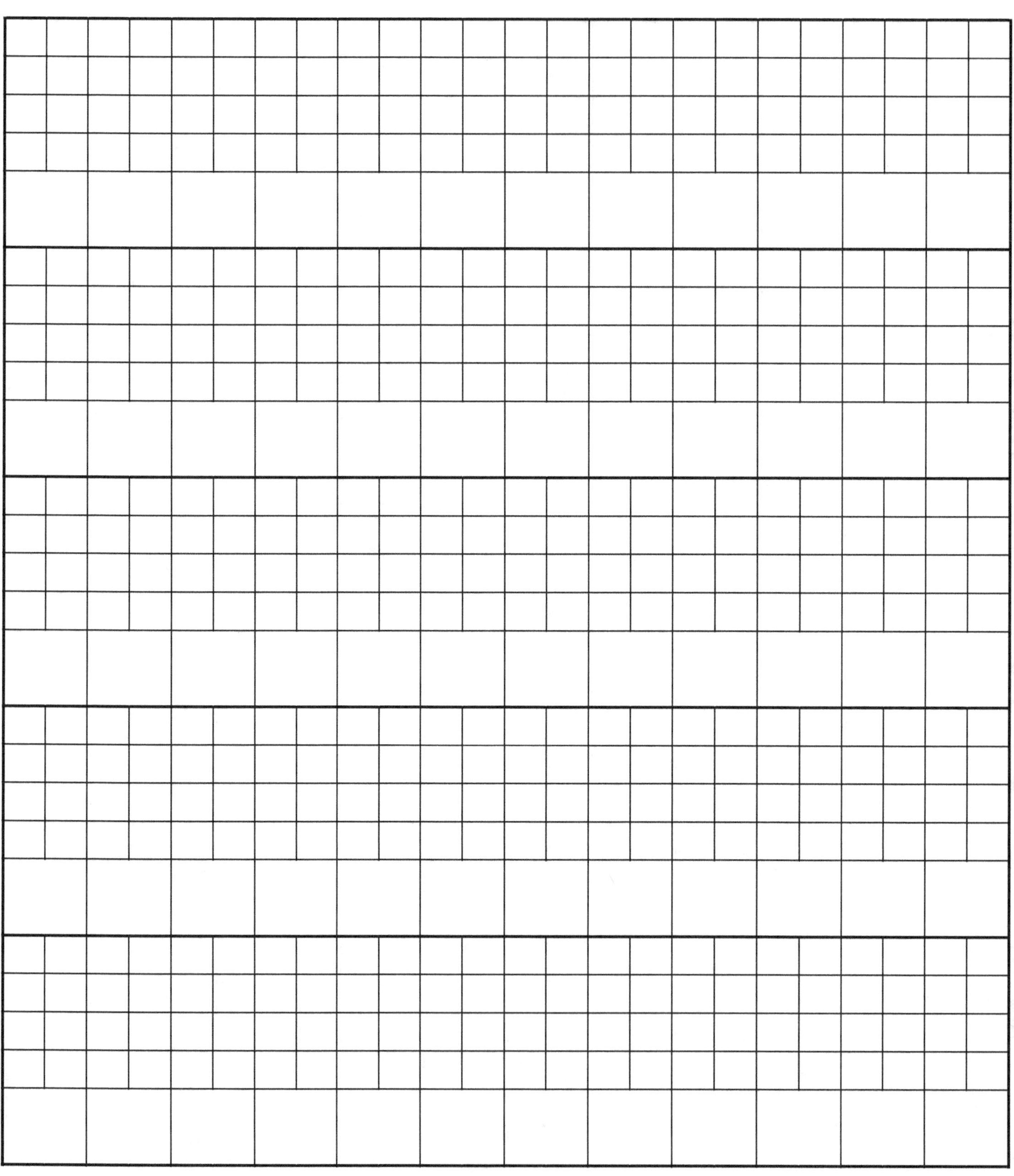

Writing Practice Sheet

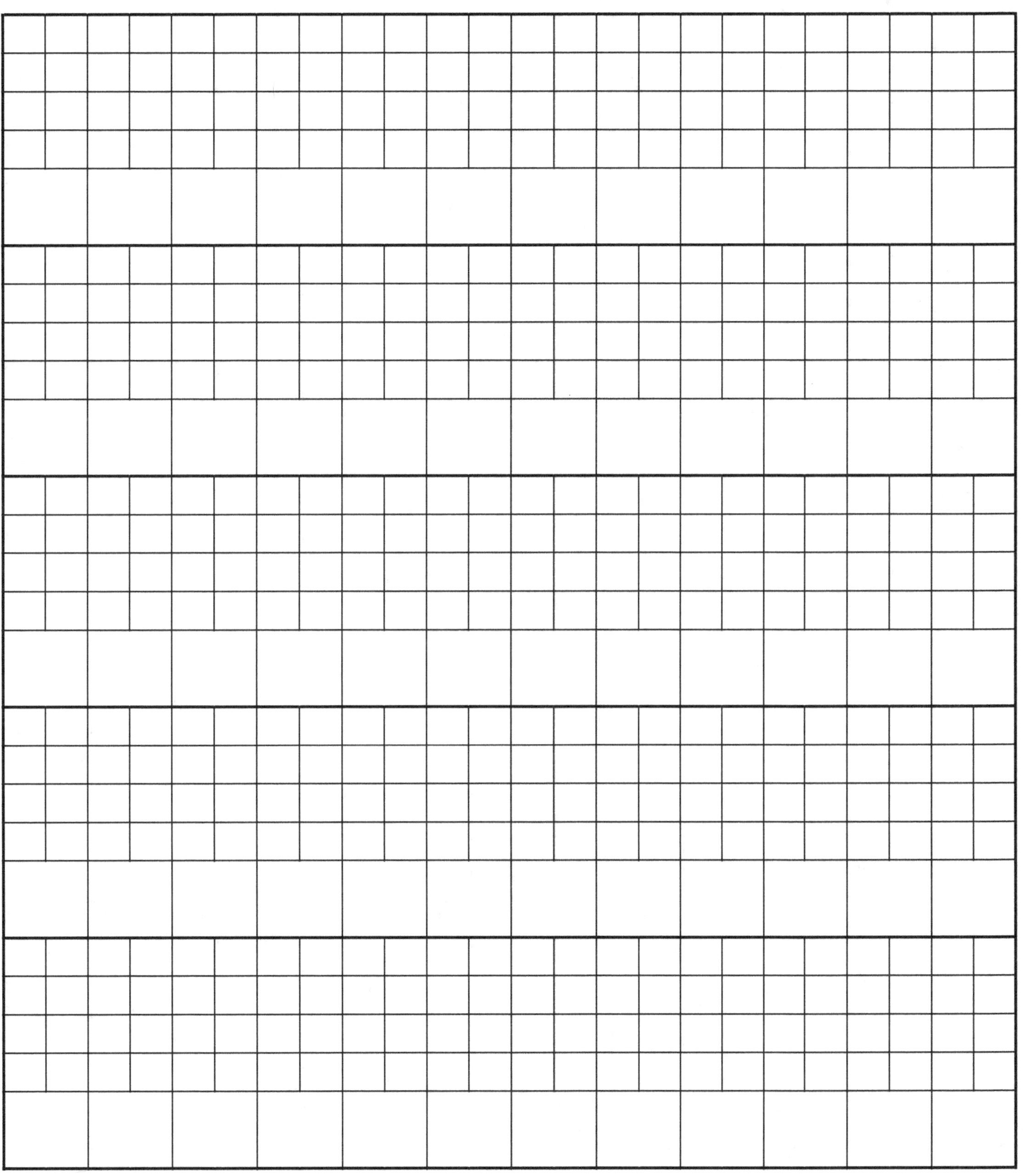

Writing Practice Sheet

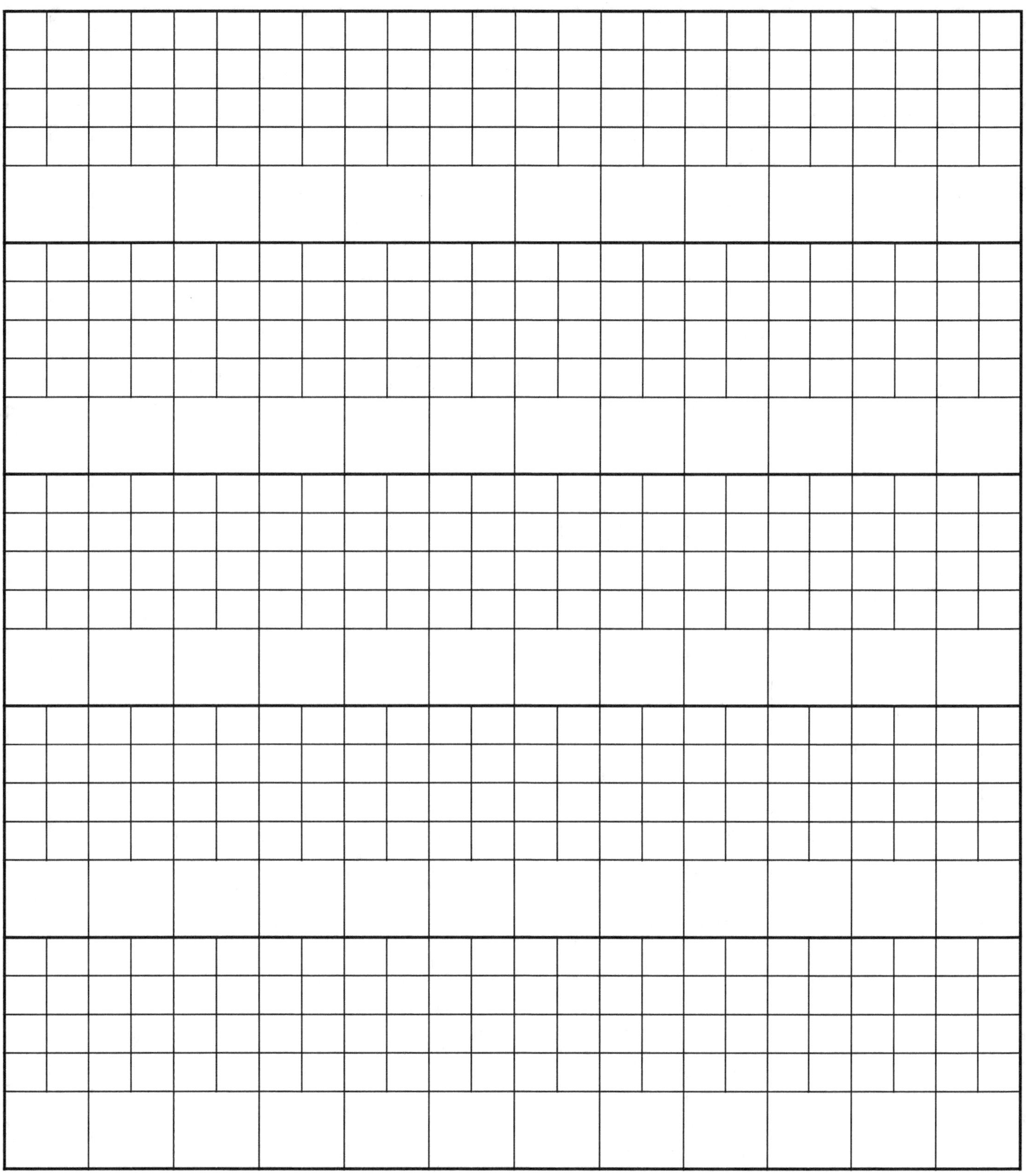

Writing Practice Sheet

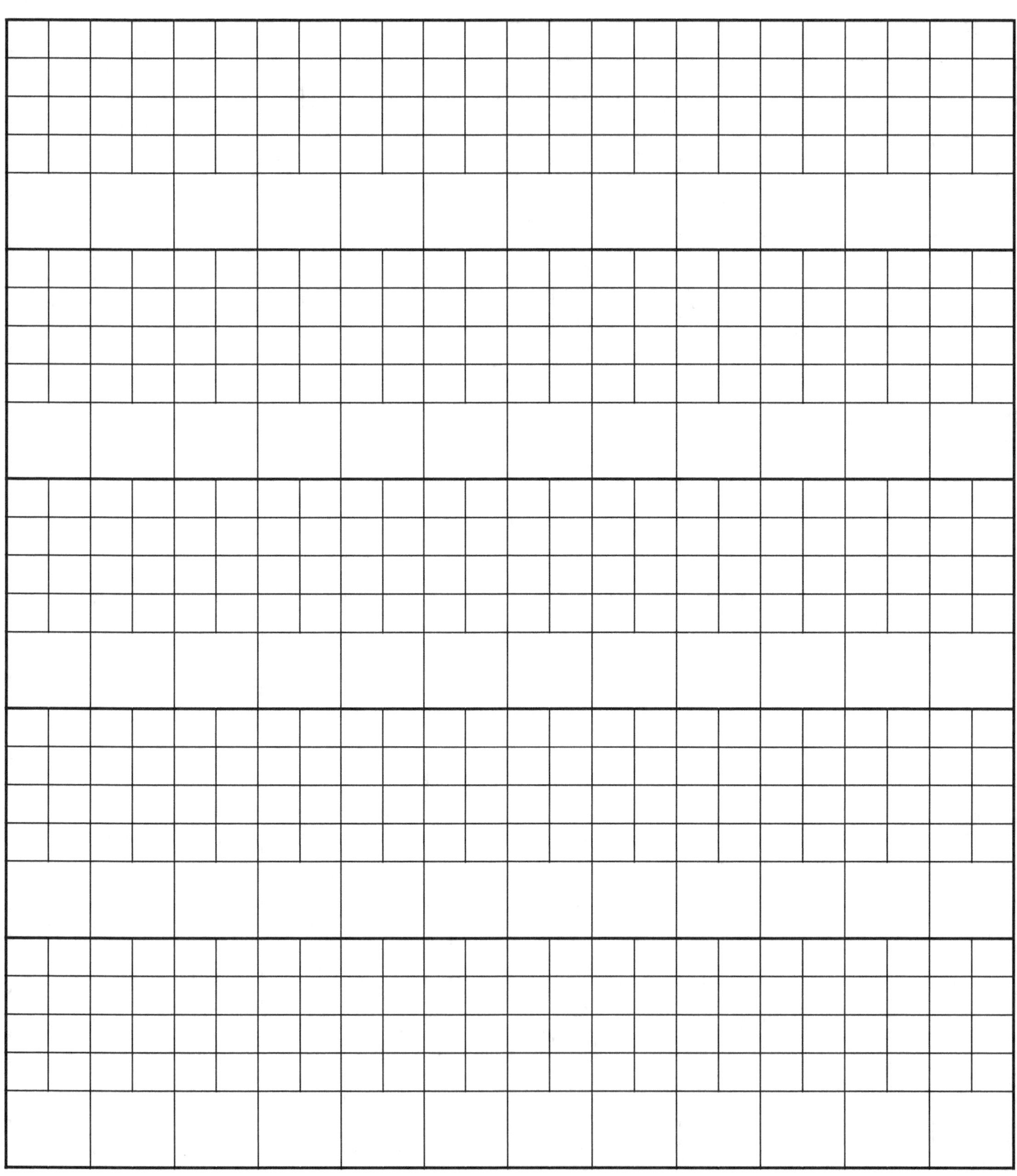

Writing Practice Sheet

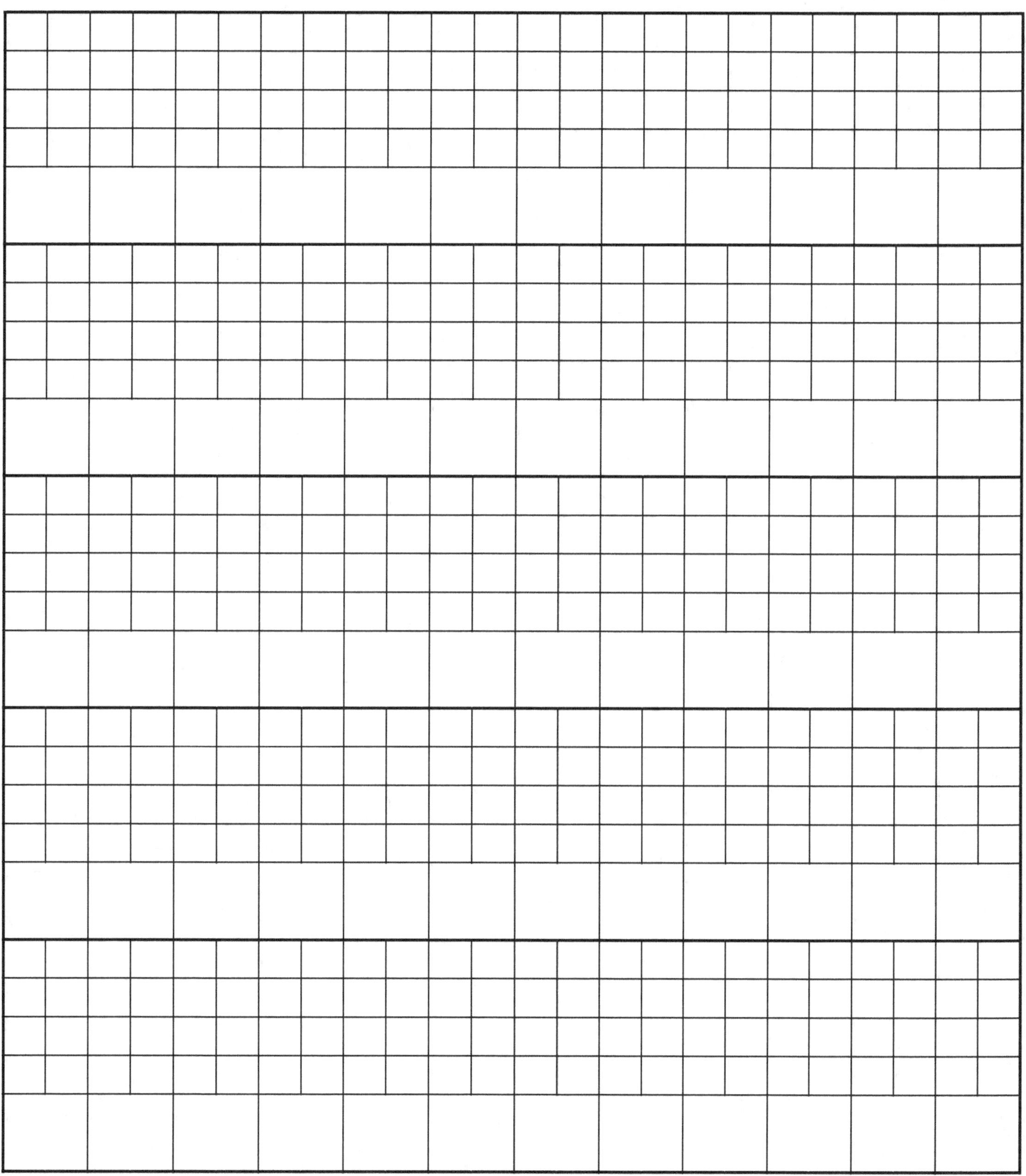

Writing Practice Sheet

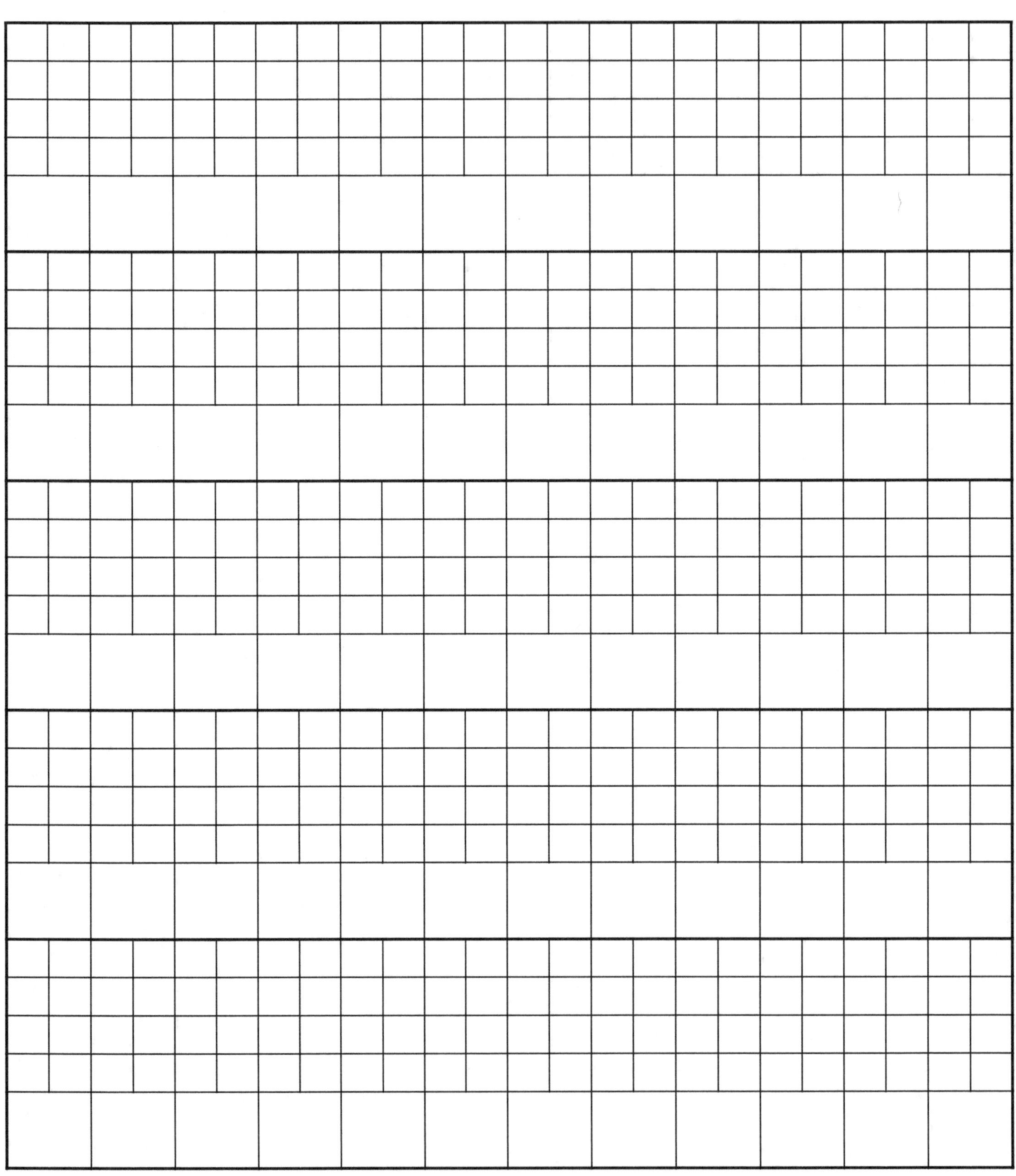

Writing Practice Sheet

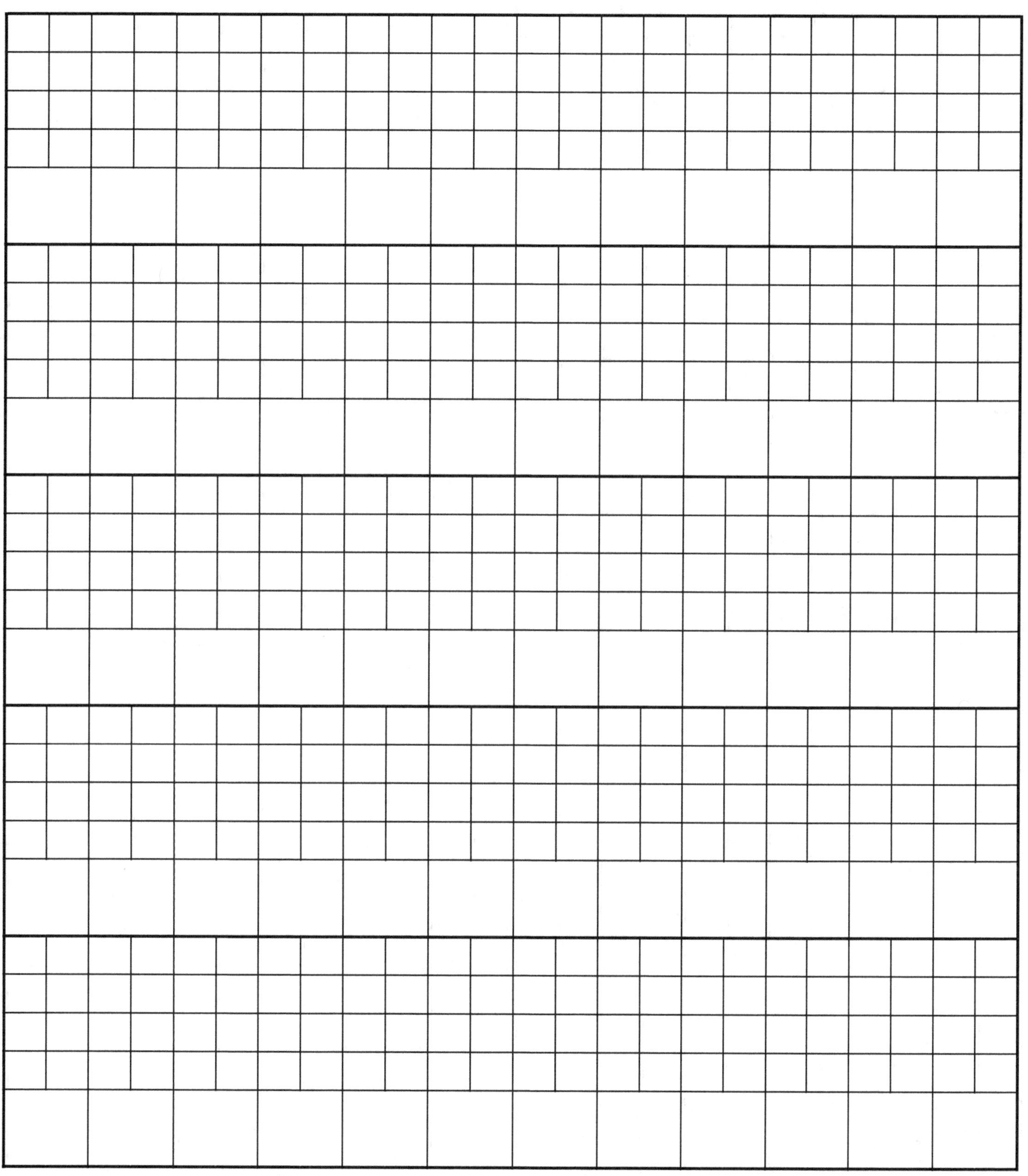

Writing Practice Sheet

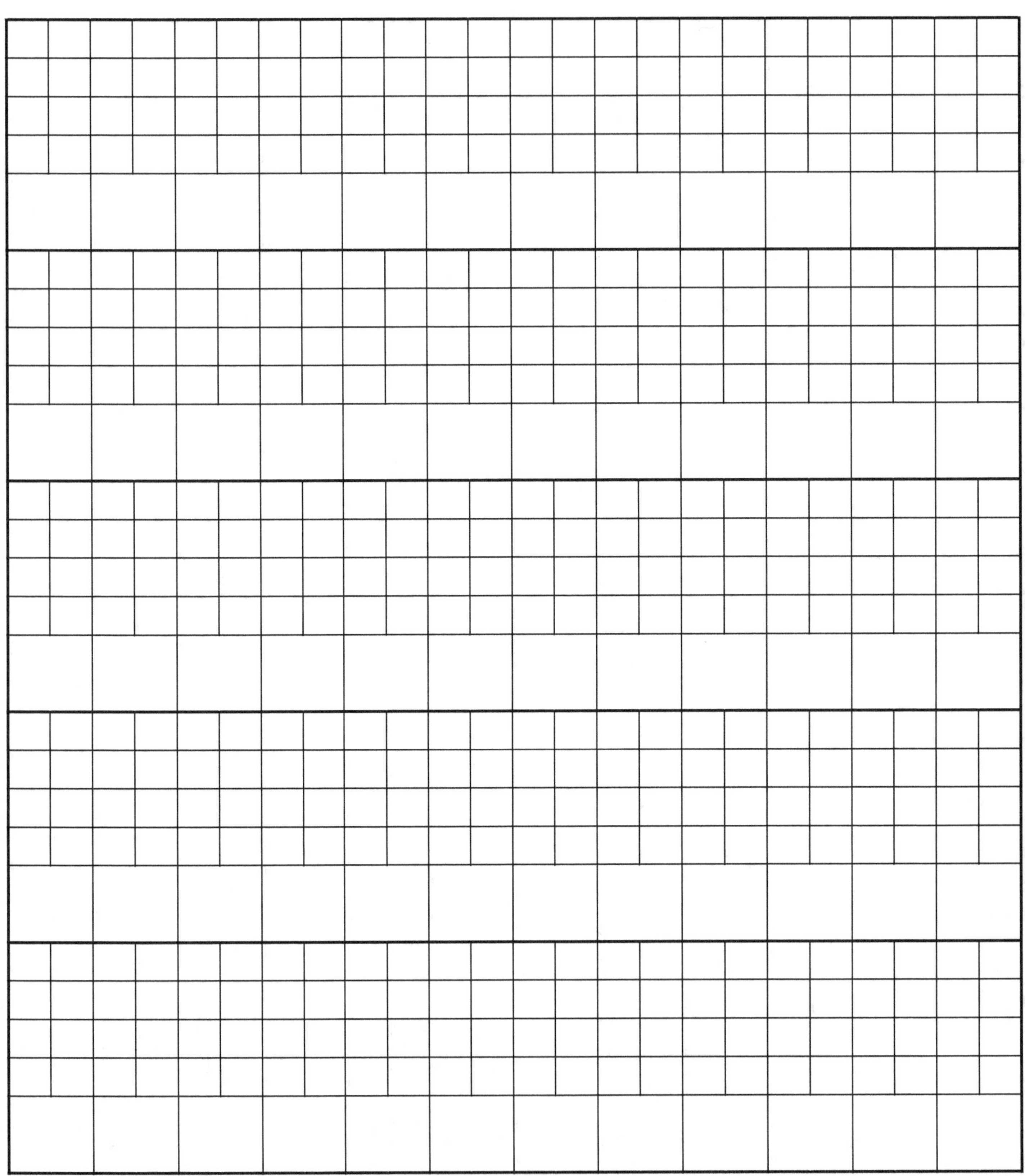

Writing Practice Sheet

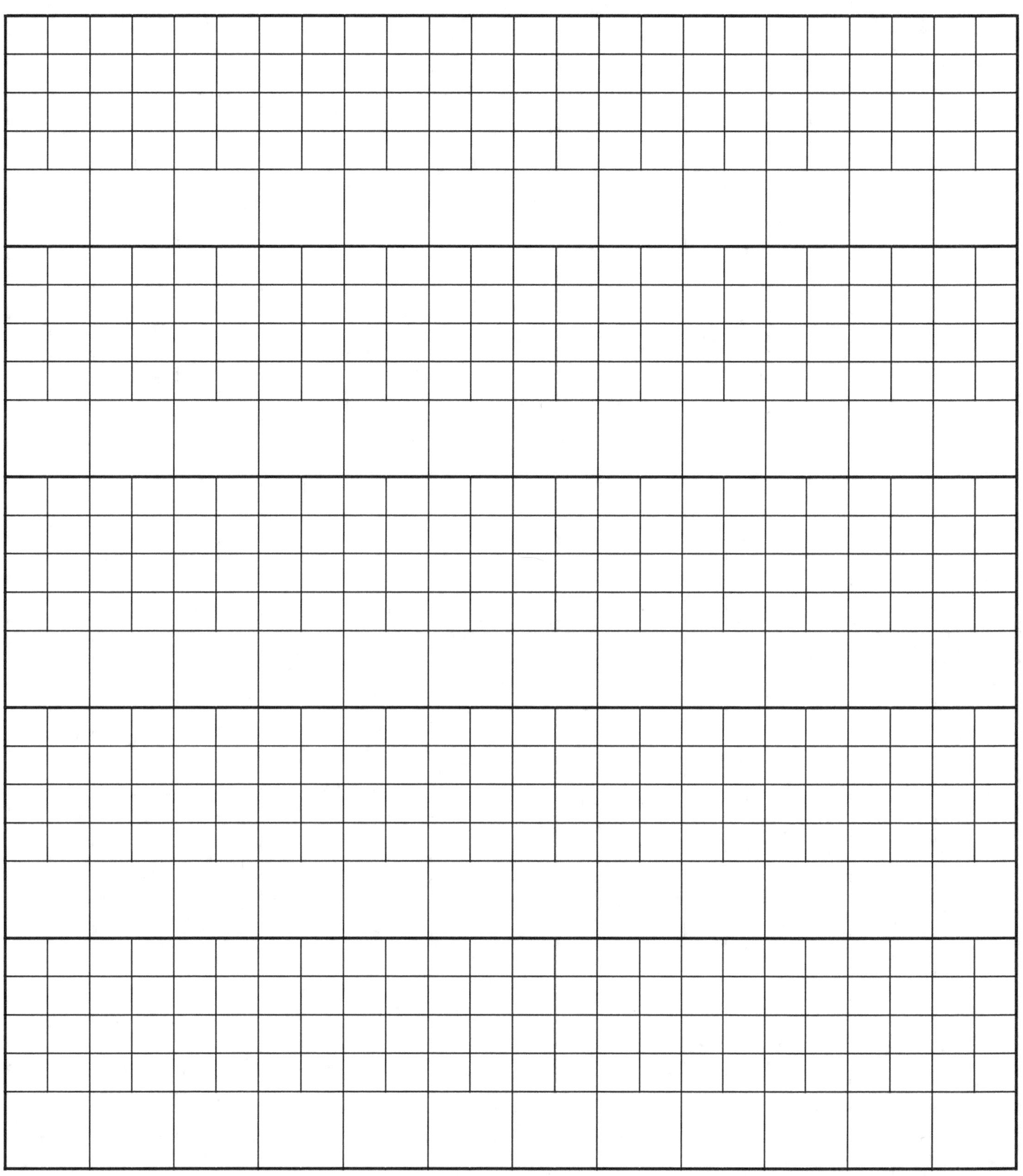

Writing Practice Sheet

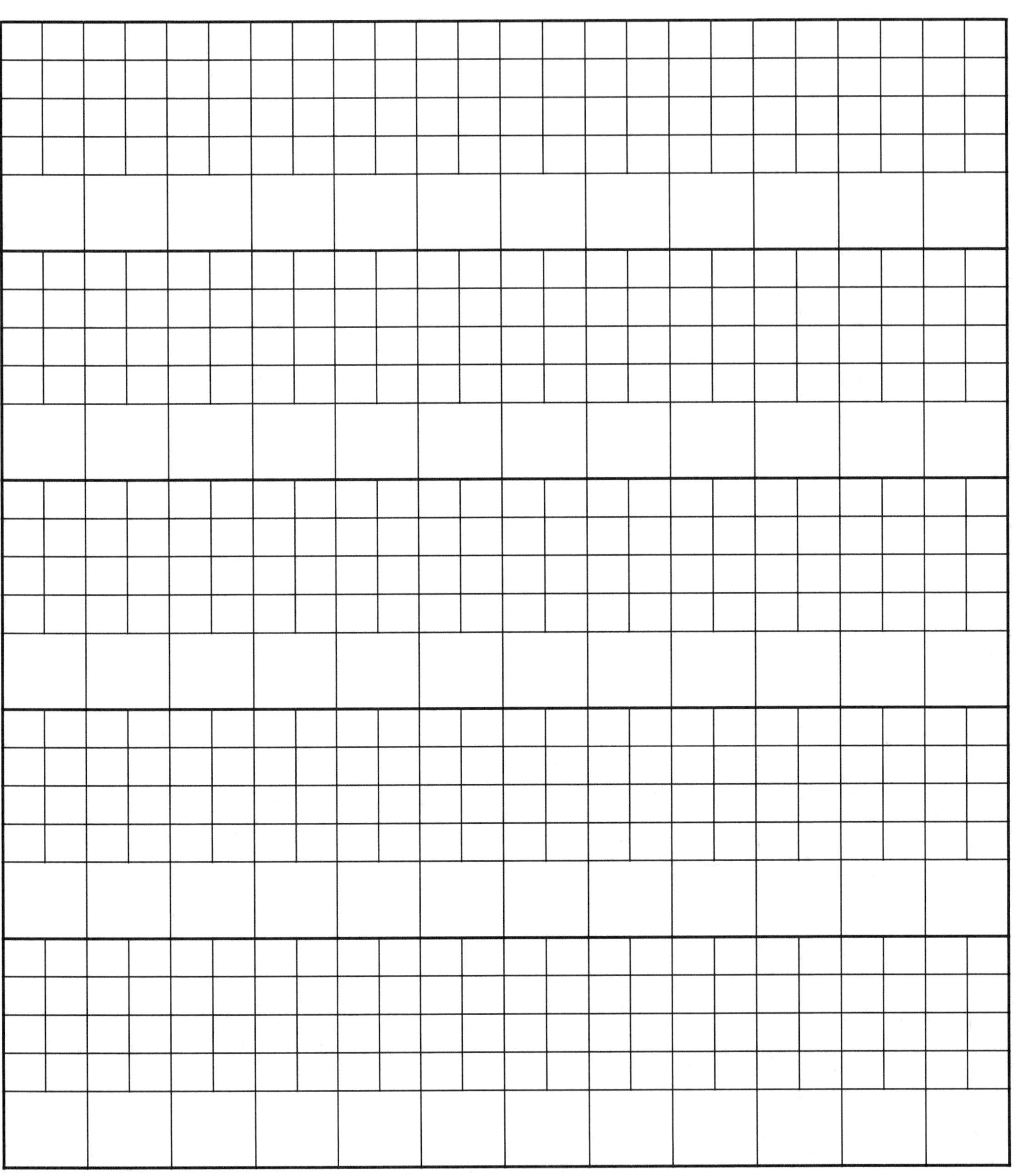

Writing Practice Sheet

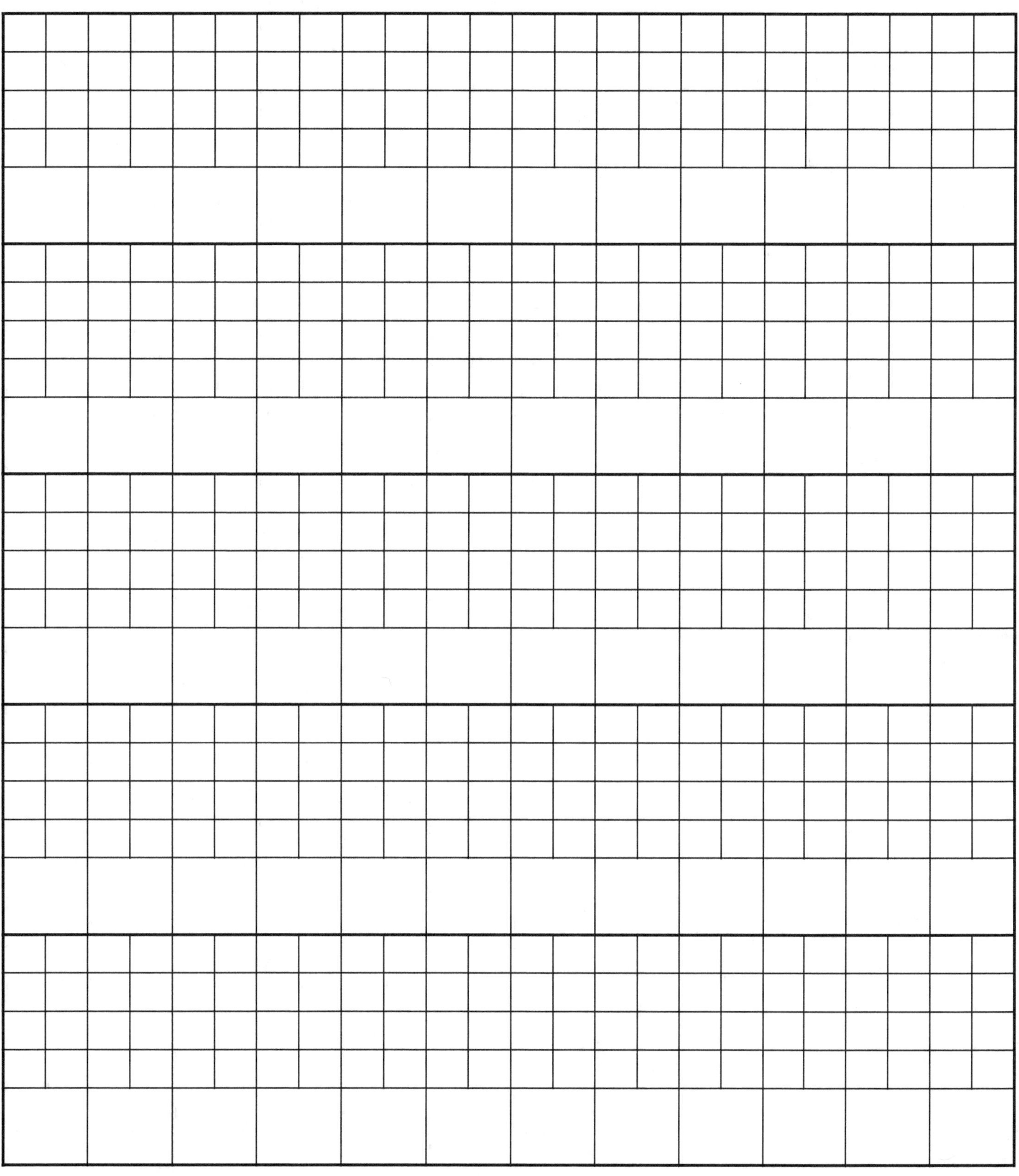

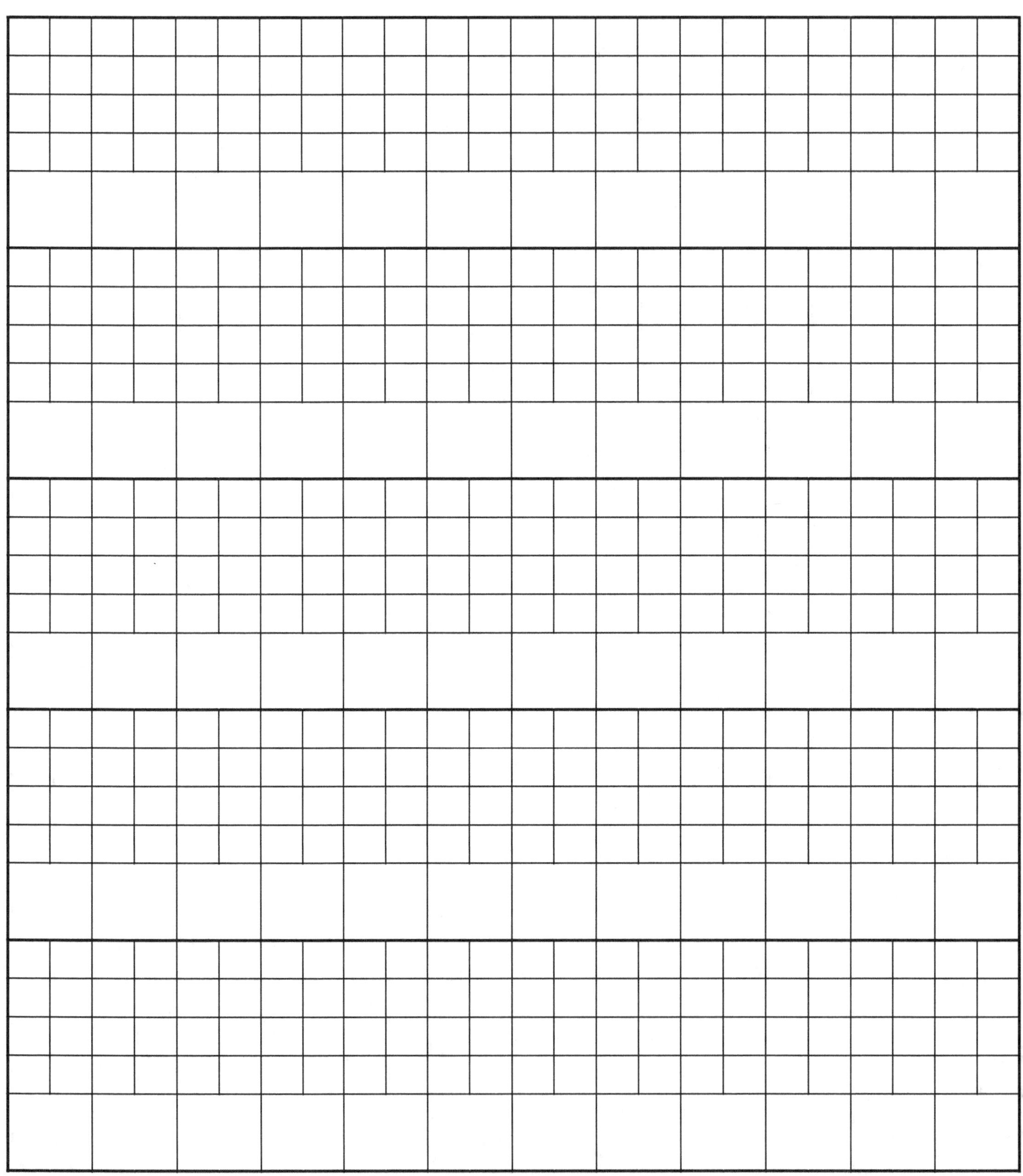

Writing Practice Sheet

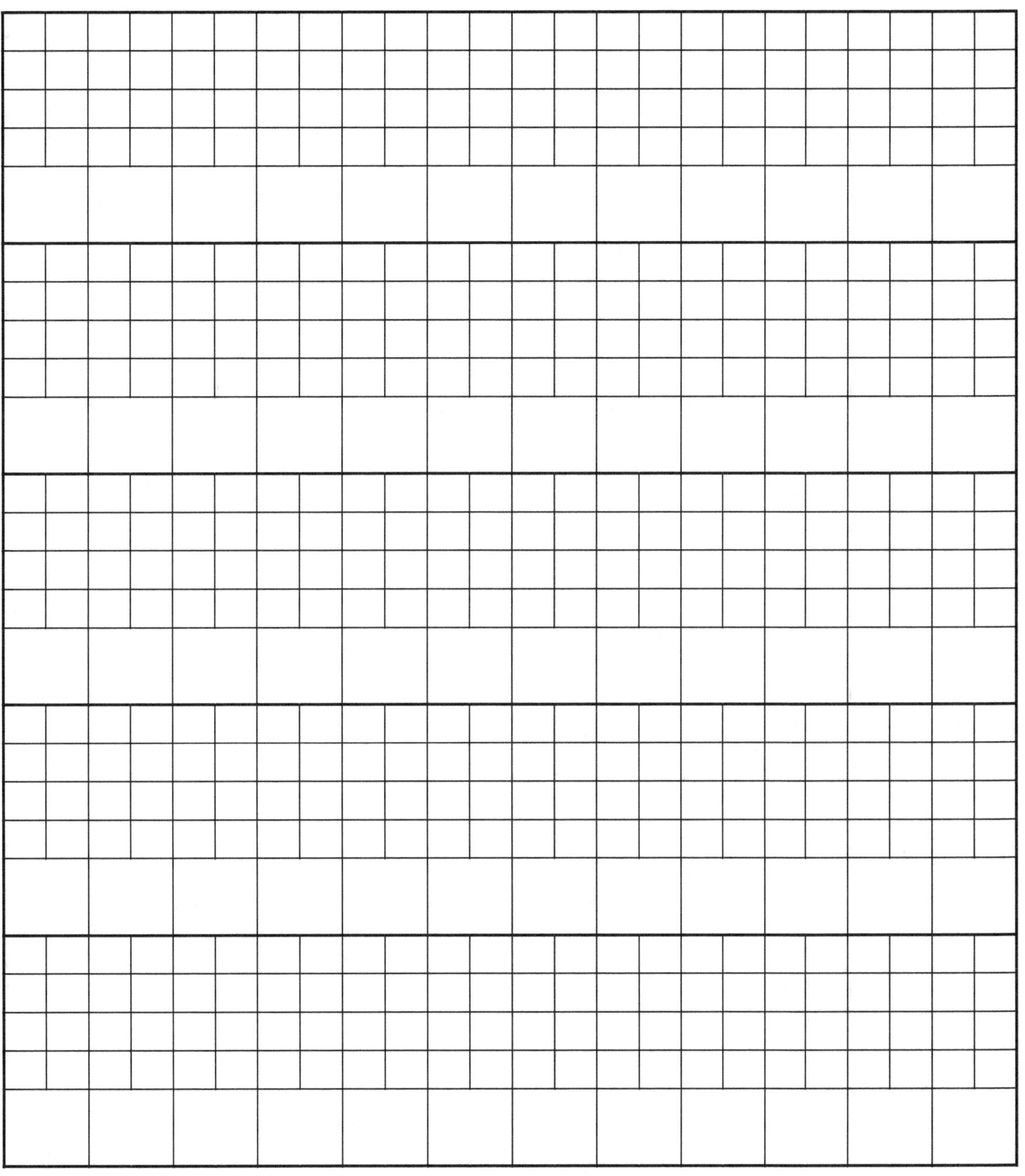

Writing Practice Sheet

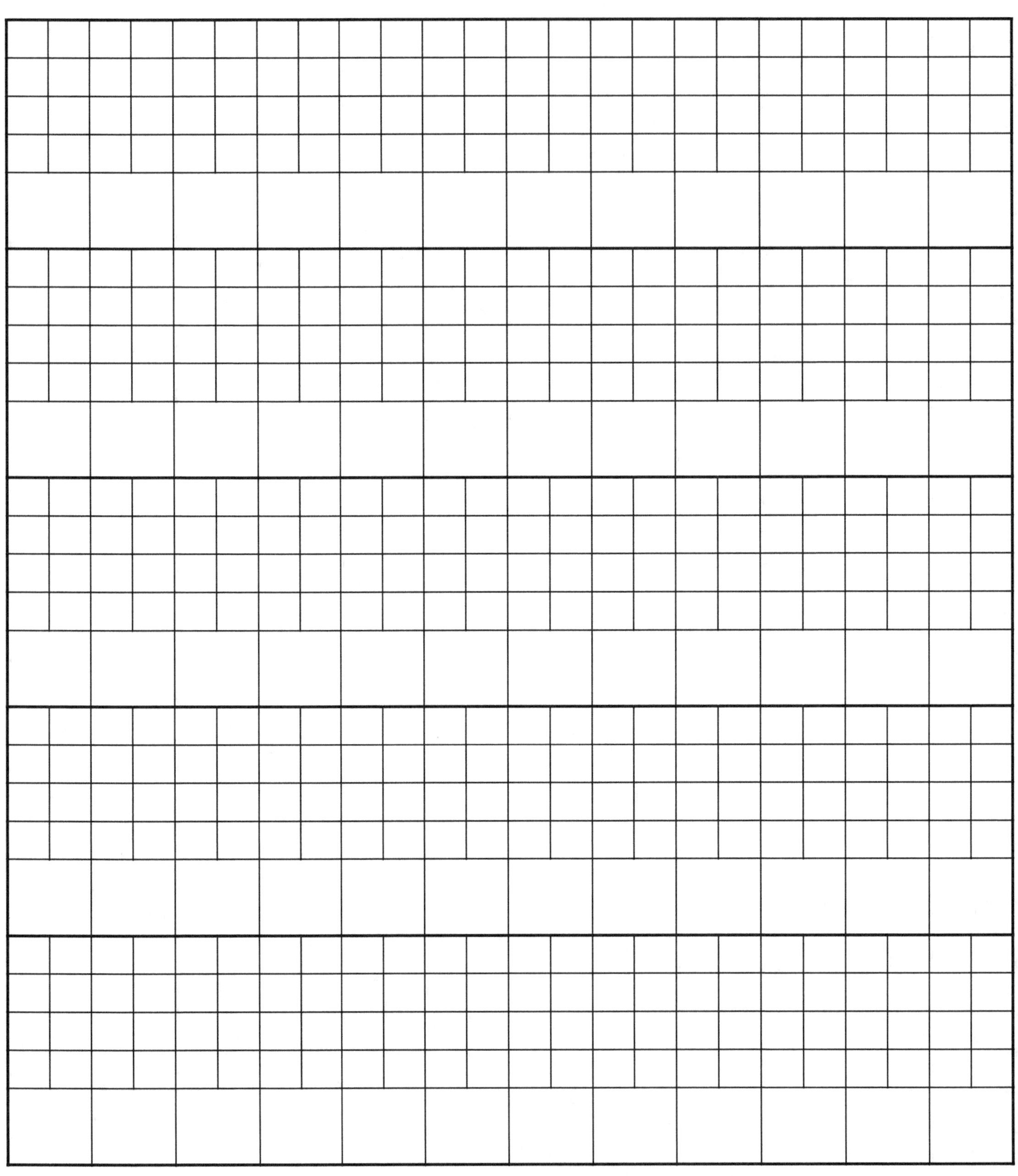

Writing Practice Sheet

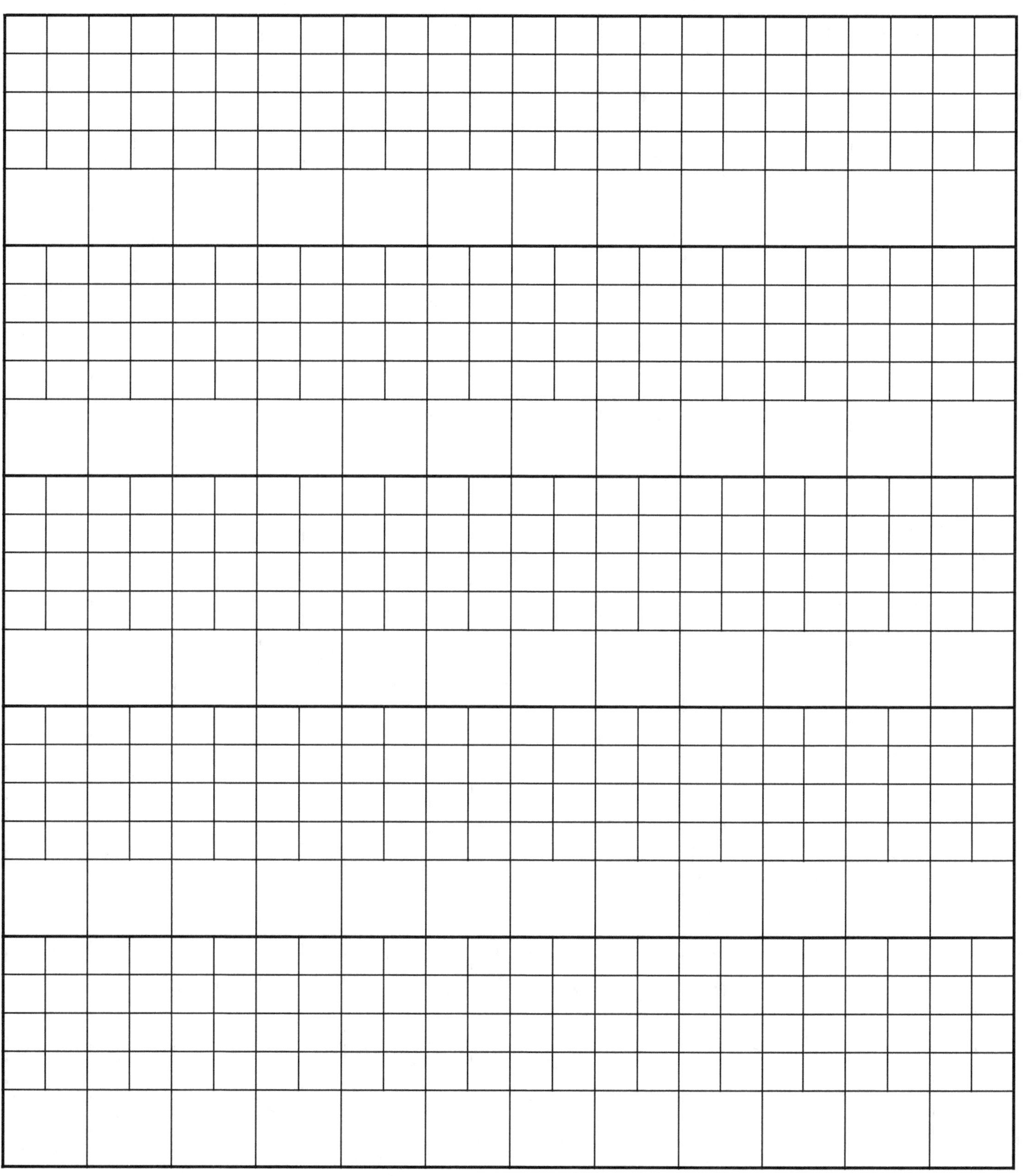

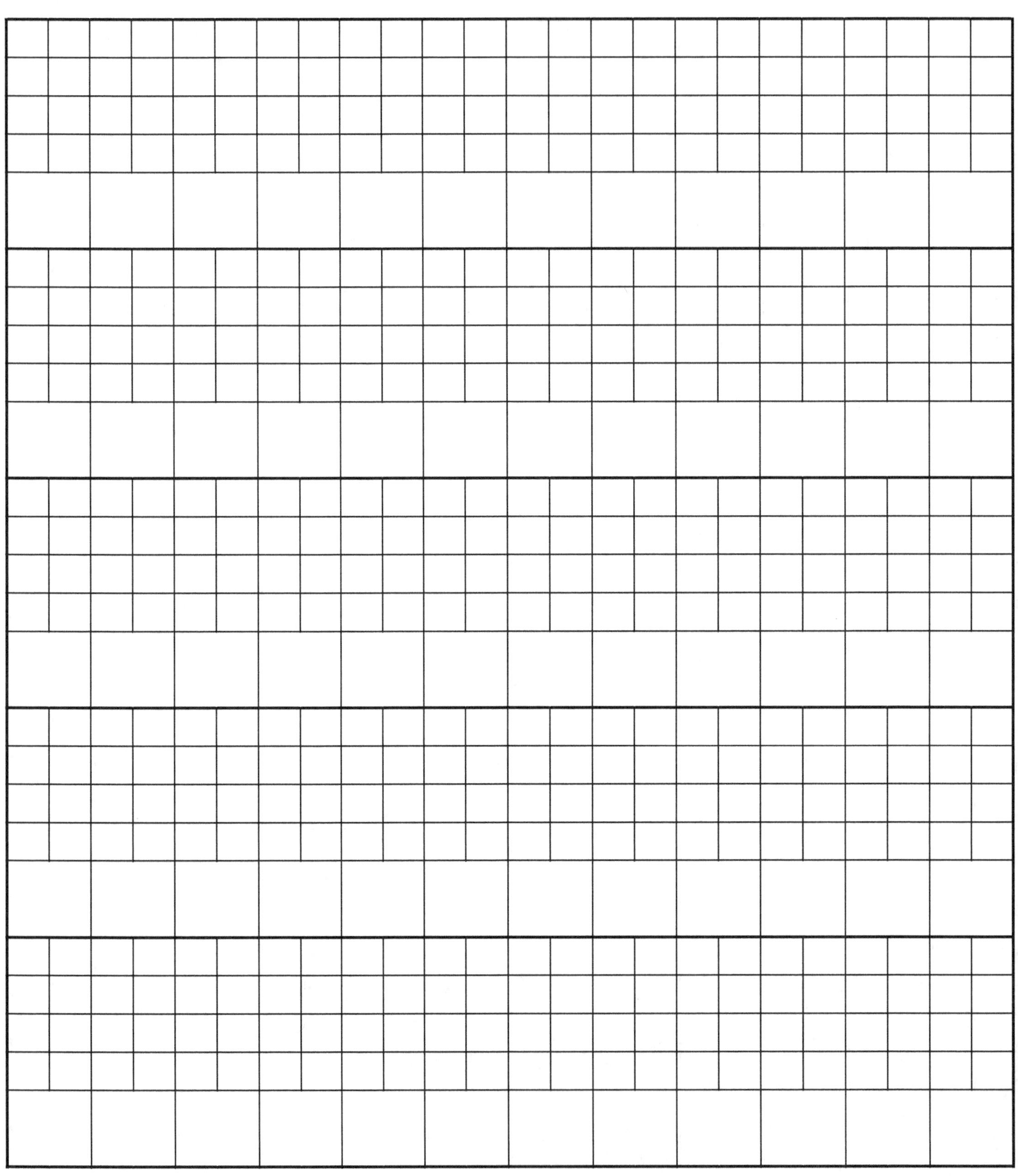

Writing Practice Sheet

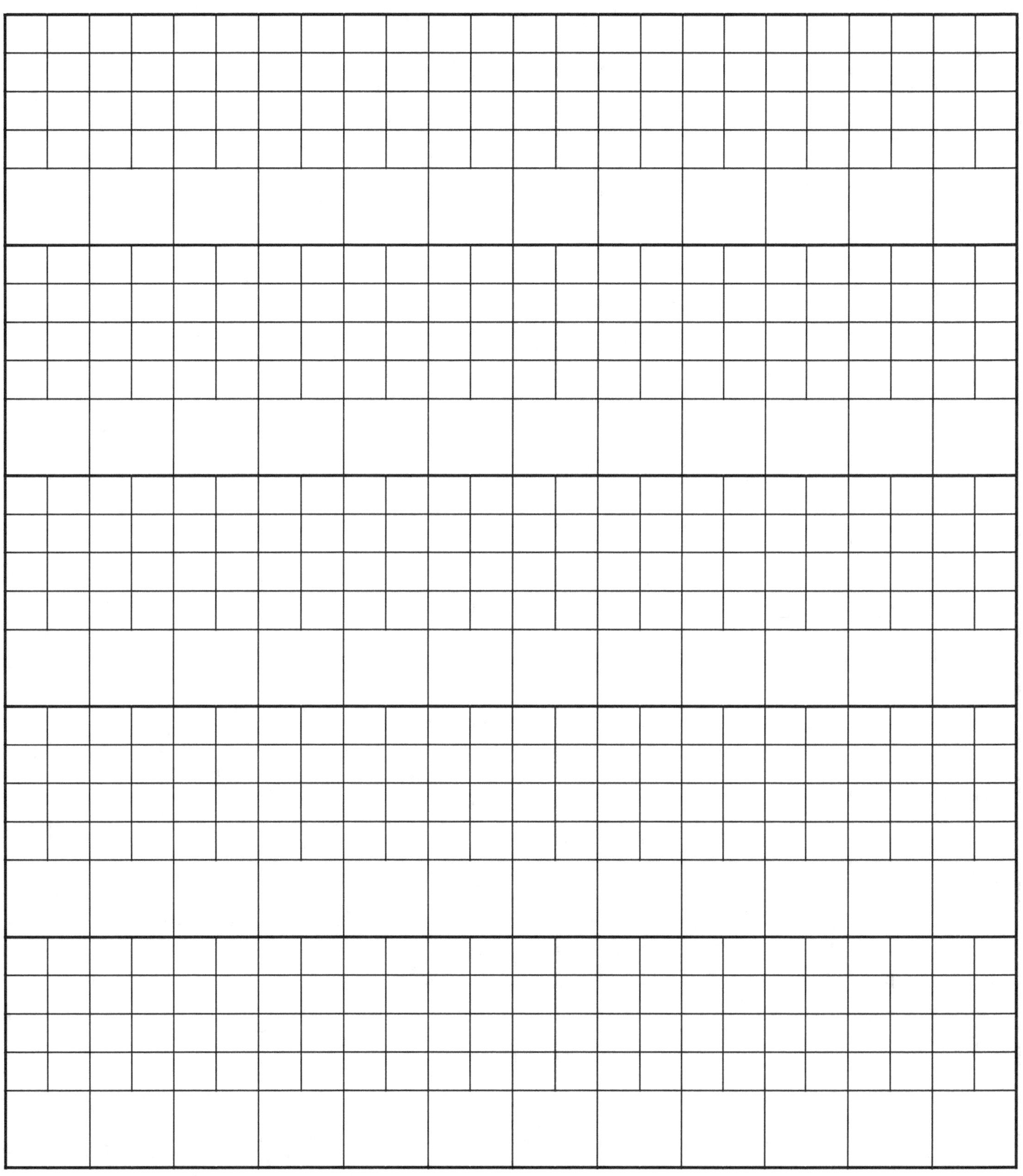

Writing Practice Sheet

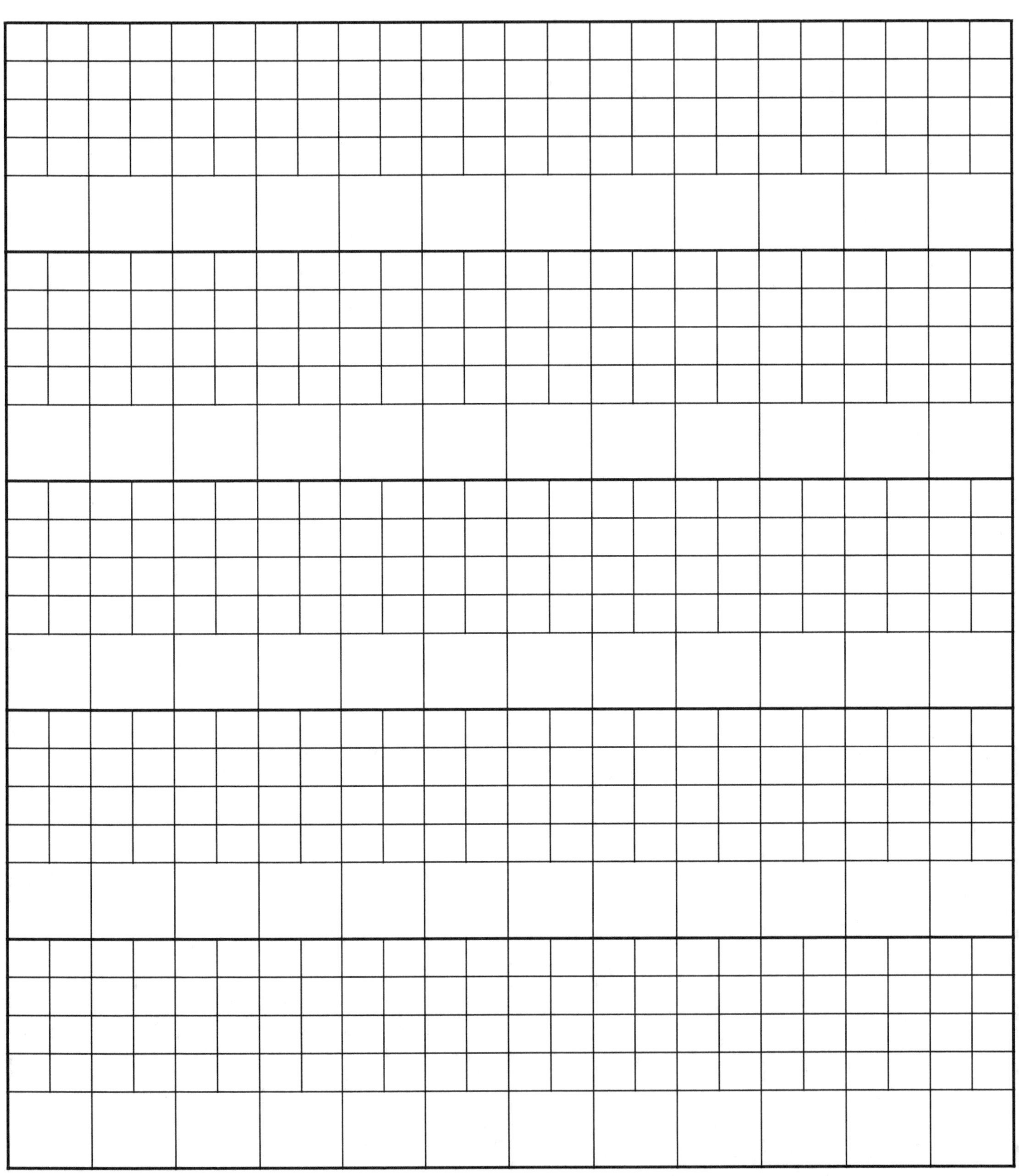

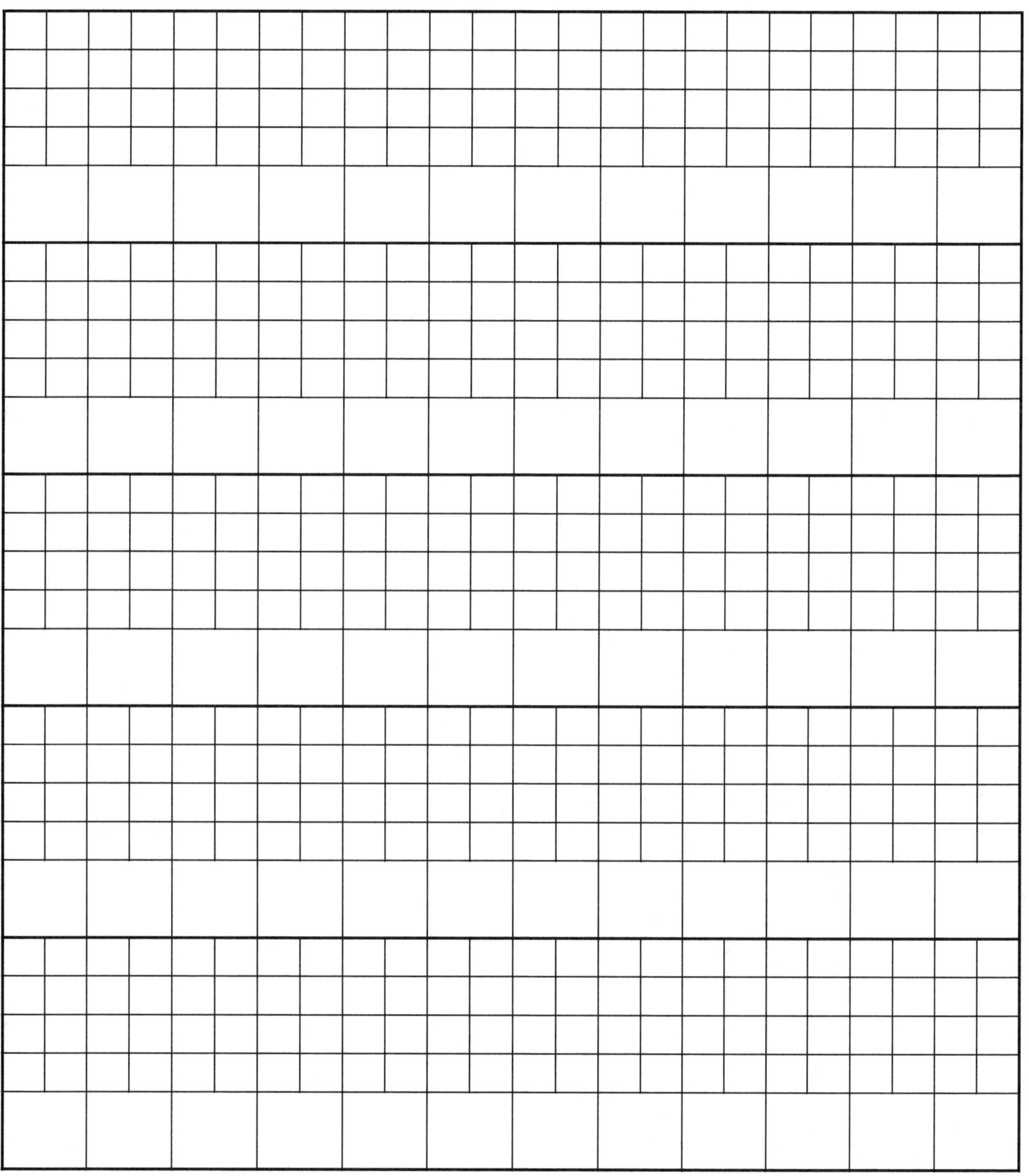

Writing Practice Sheet

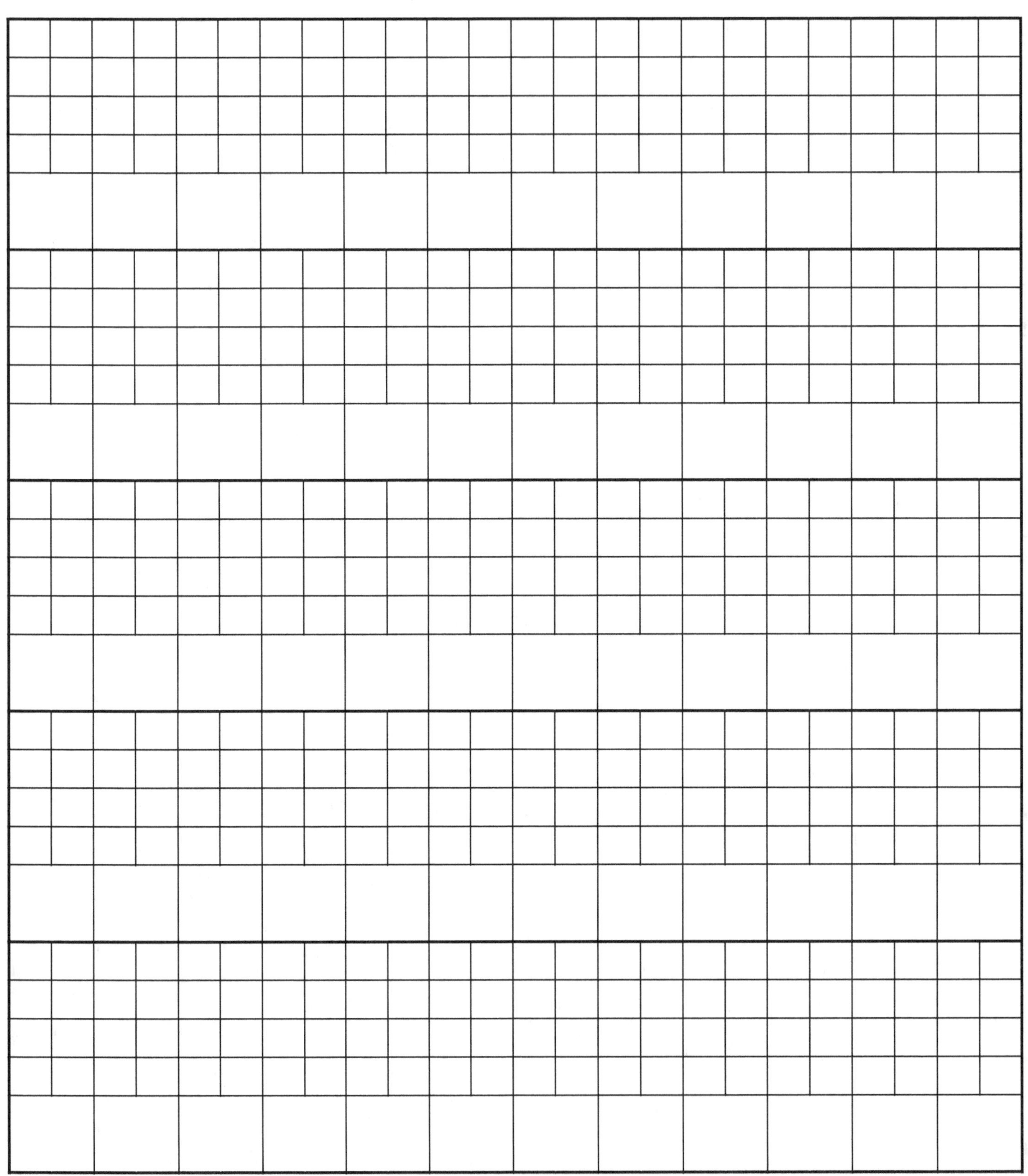

Writing Practice Sheet

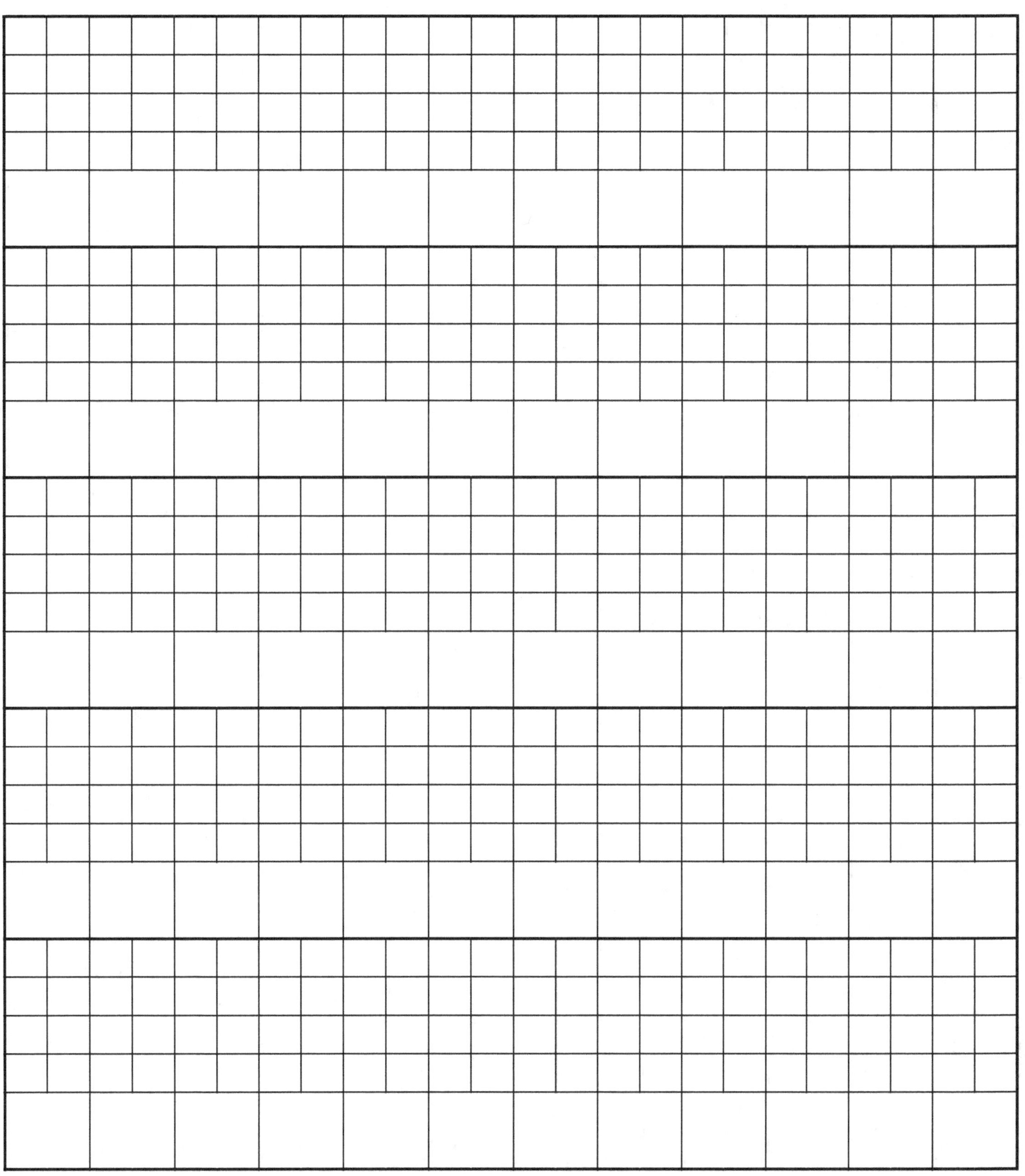

Writing Practice Sheet

Writing Practice Sheet

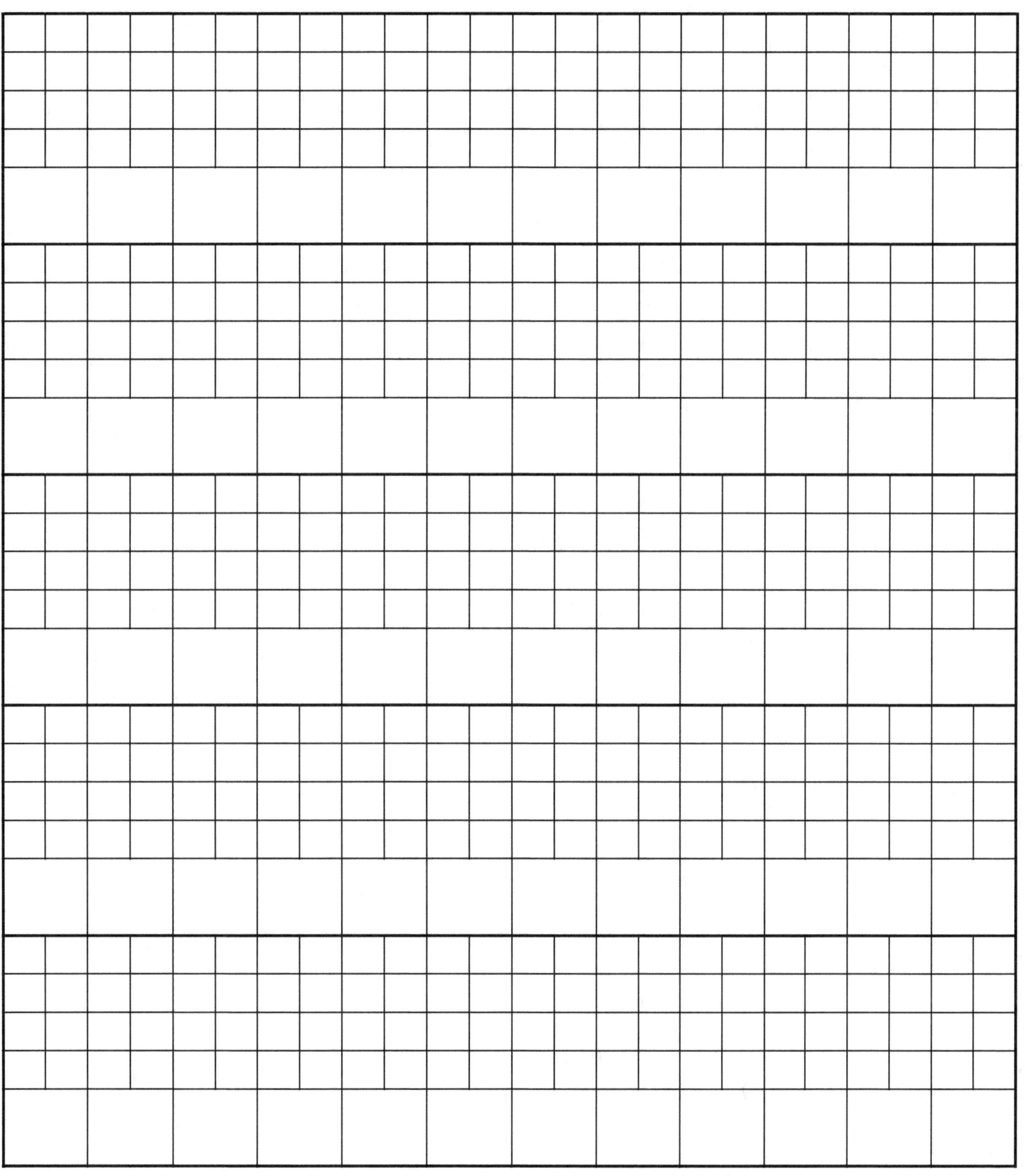

Writing Practice Sheet

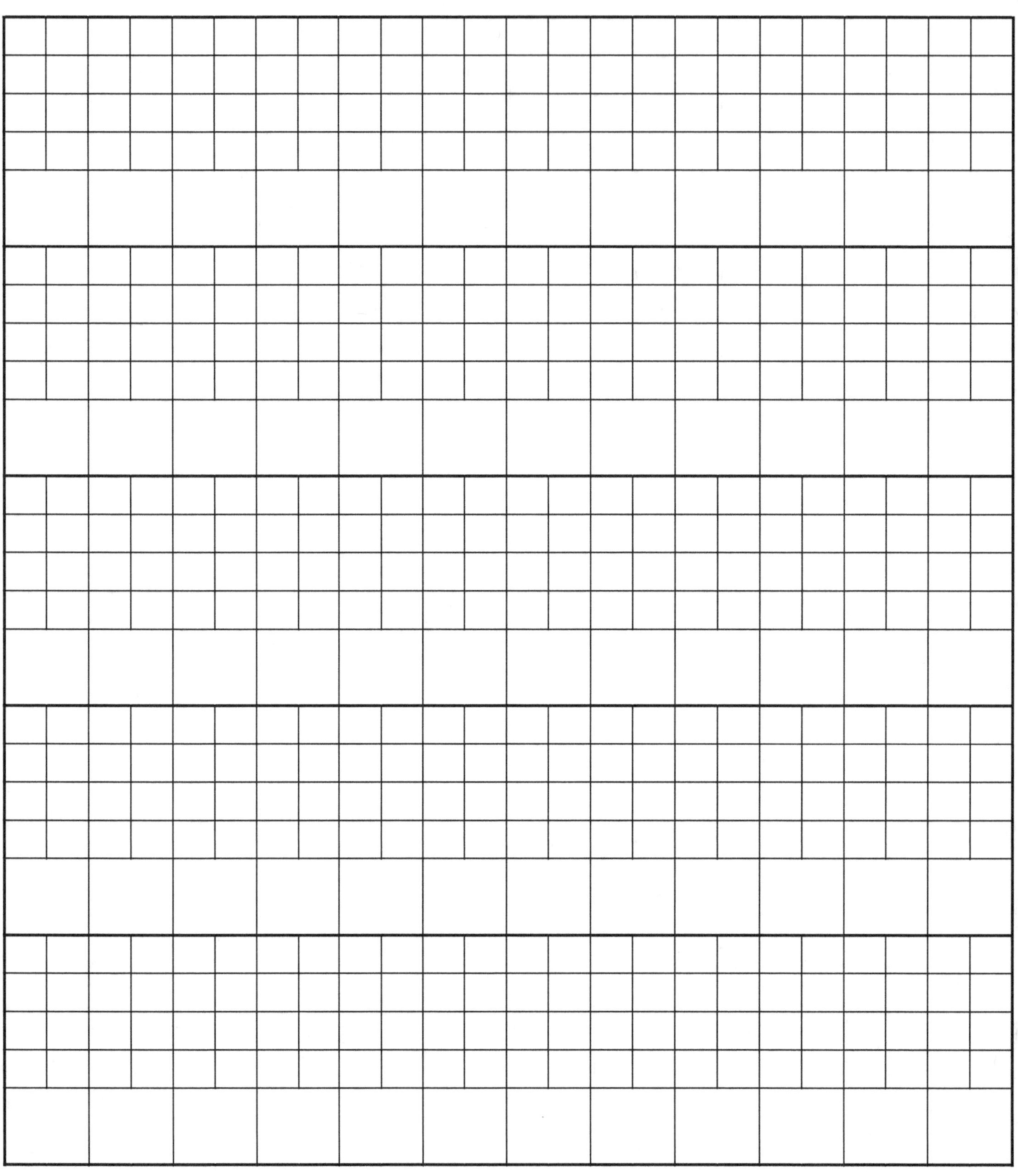

Writing Practice Sheet

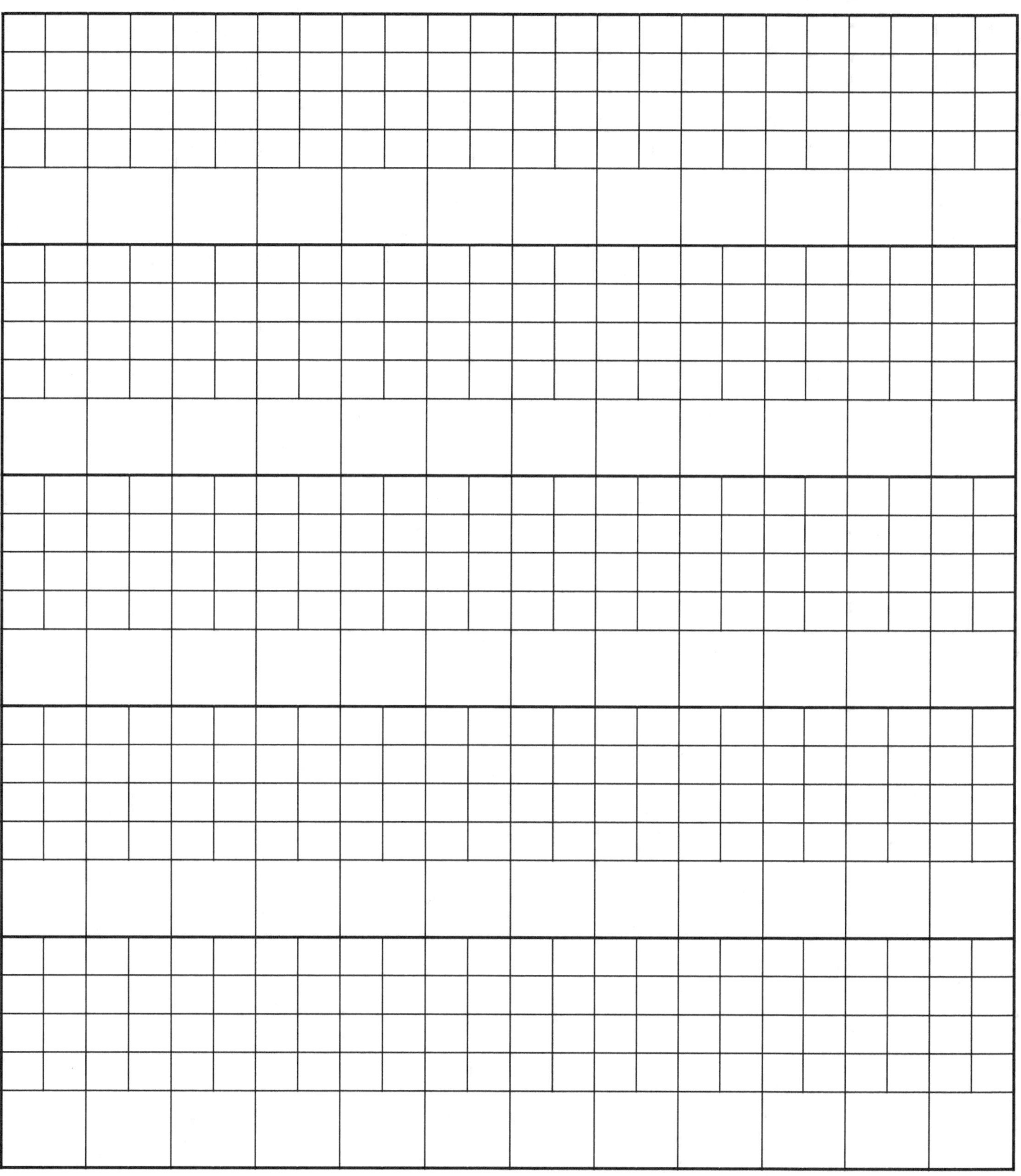

Writing Practice Sheet

Writing Practice Sheet

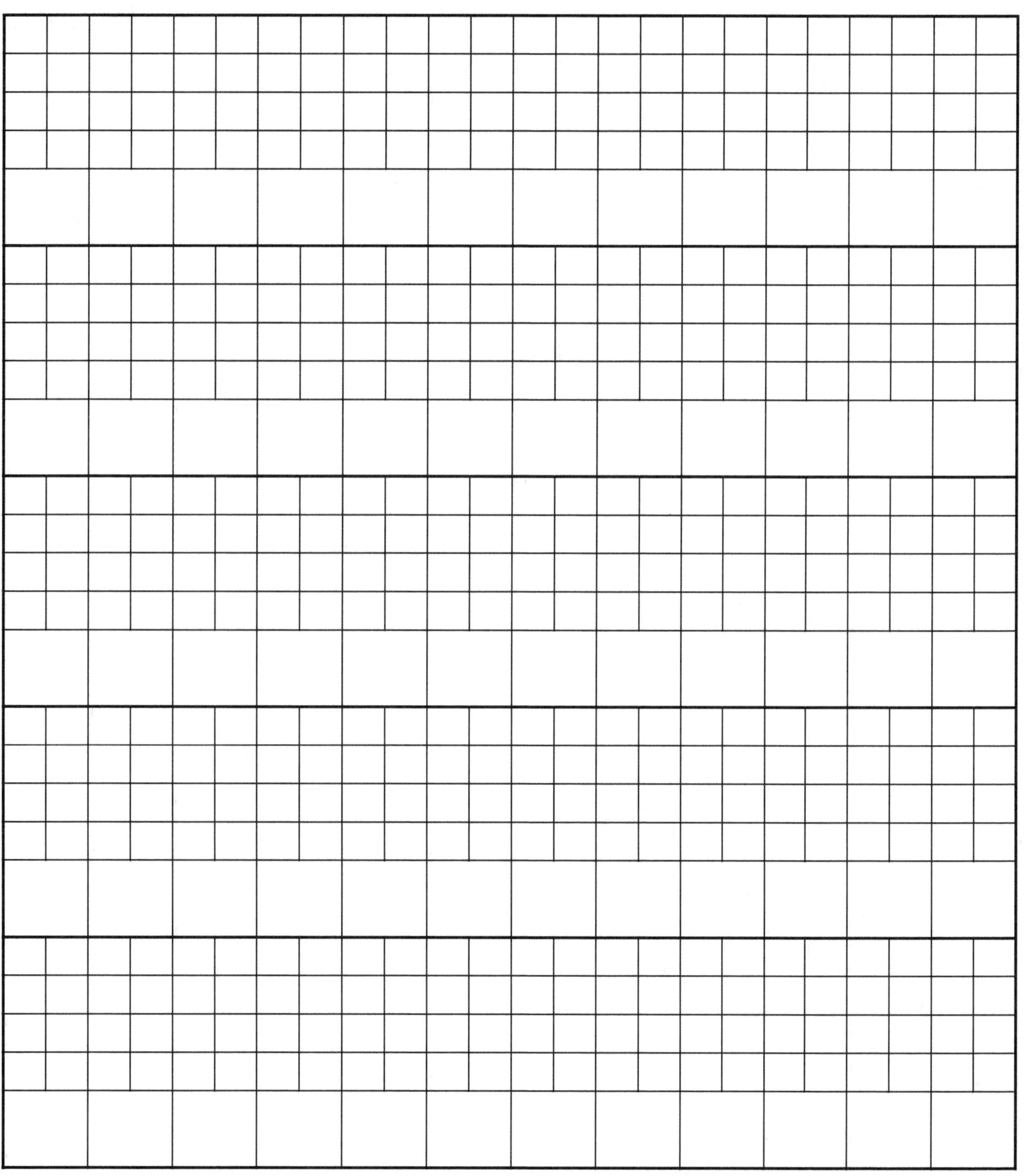

Writing Practice Sheet

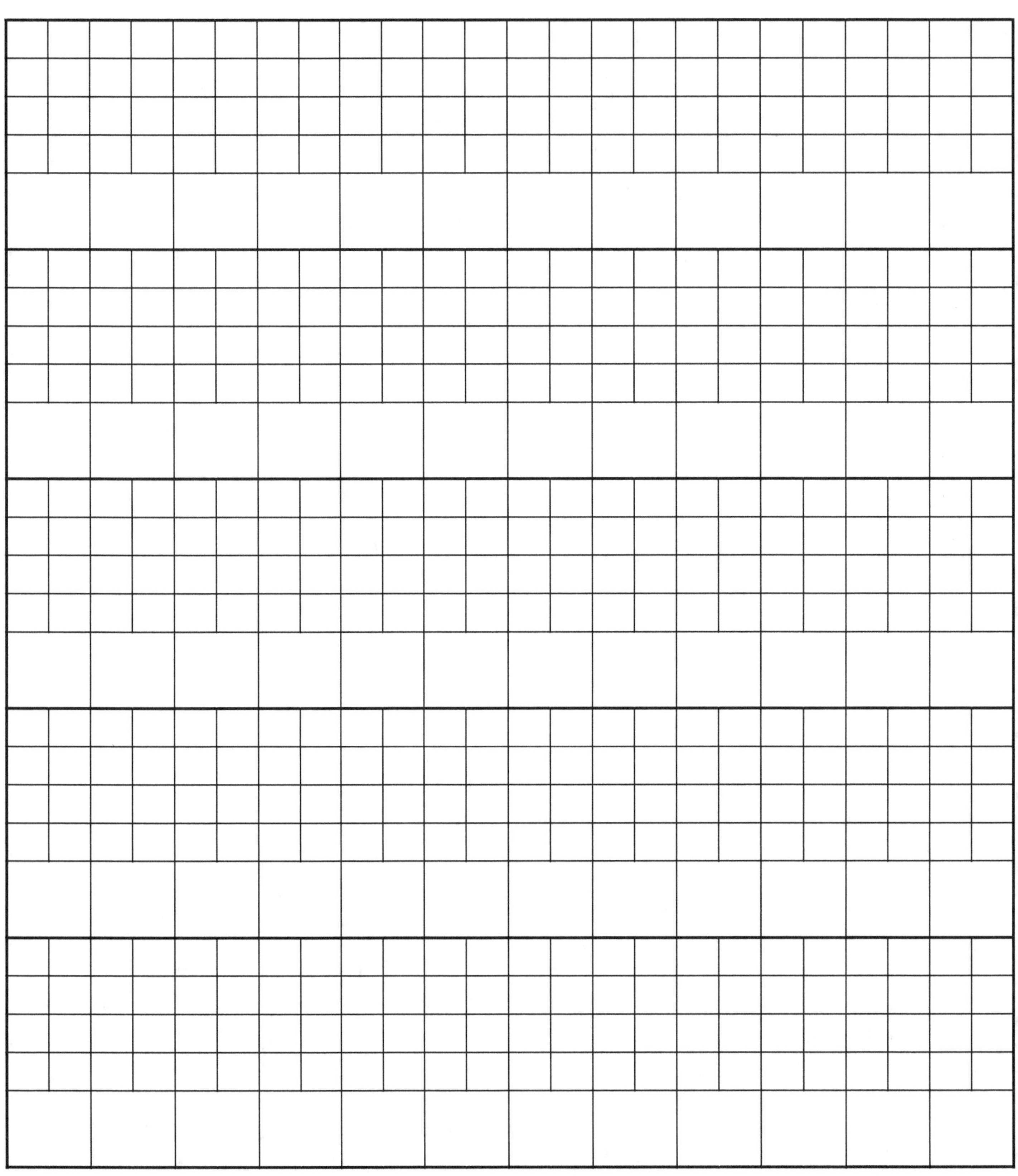

Writing Practice Sheet

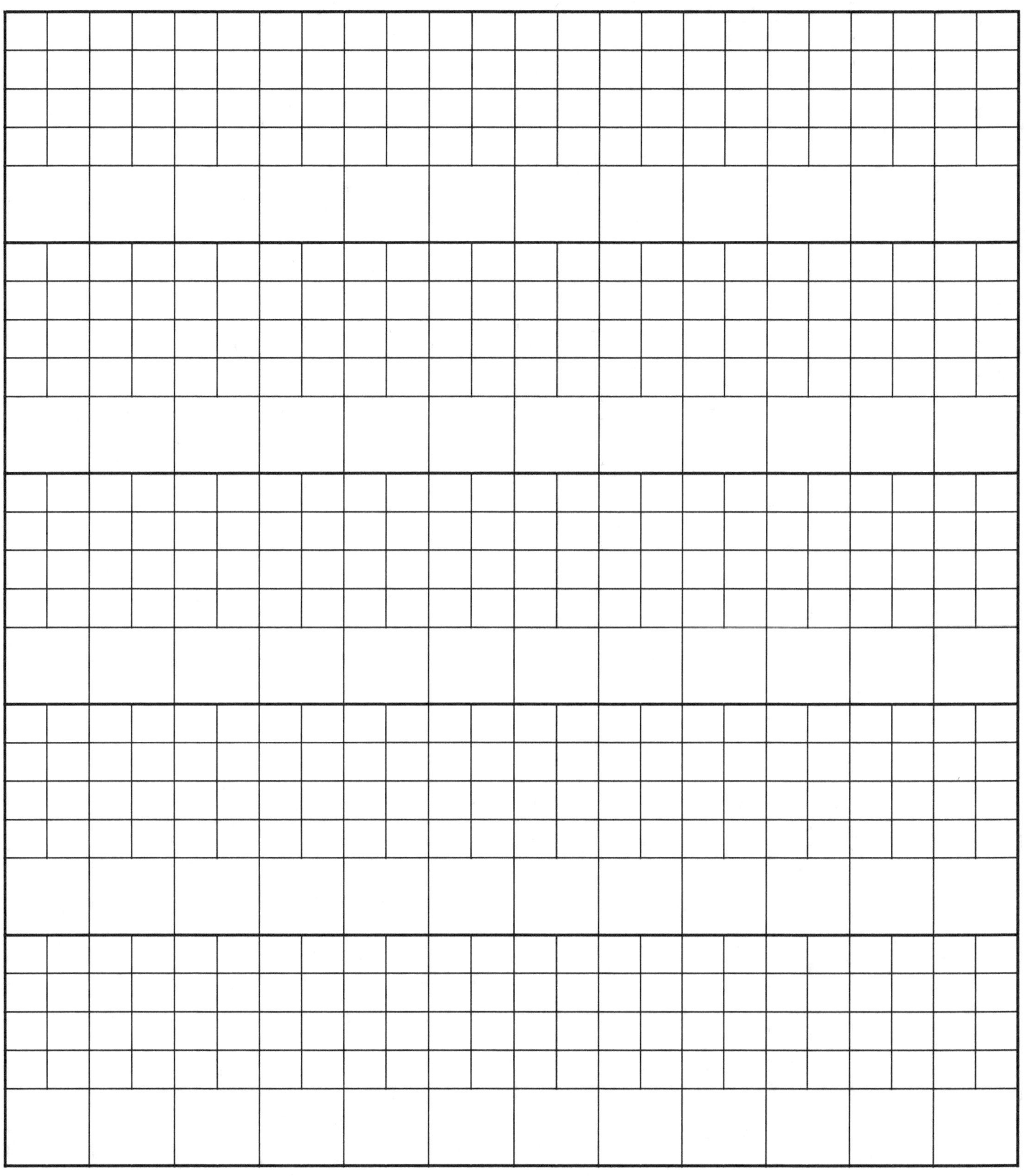

Writing Practice Sheet

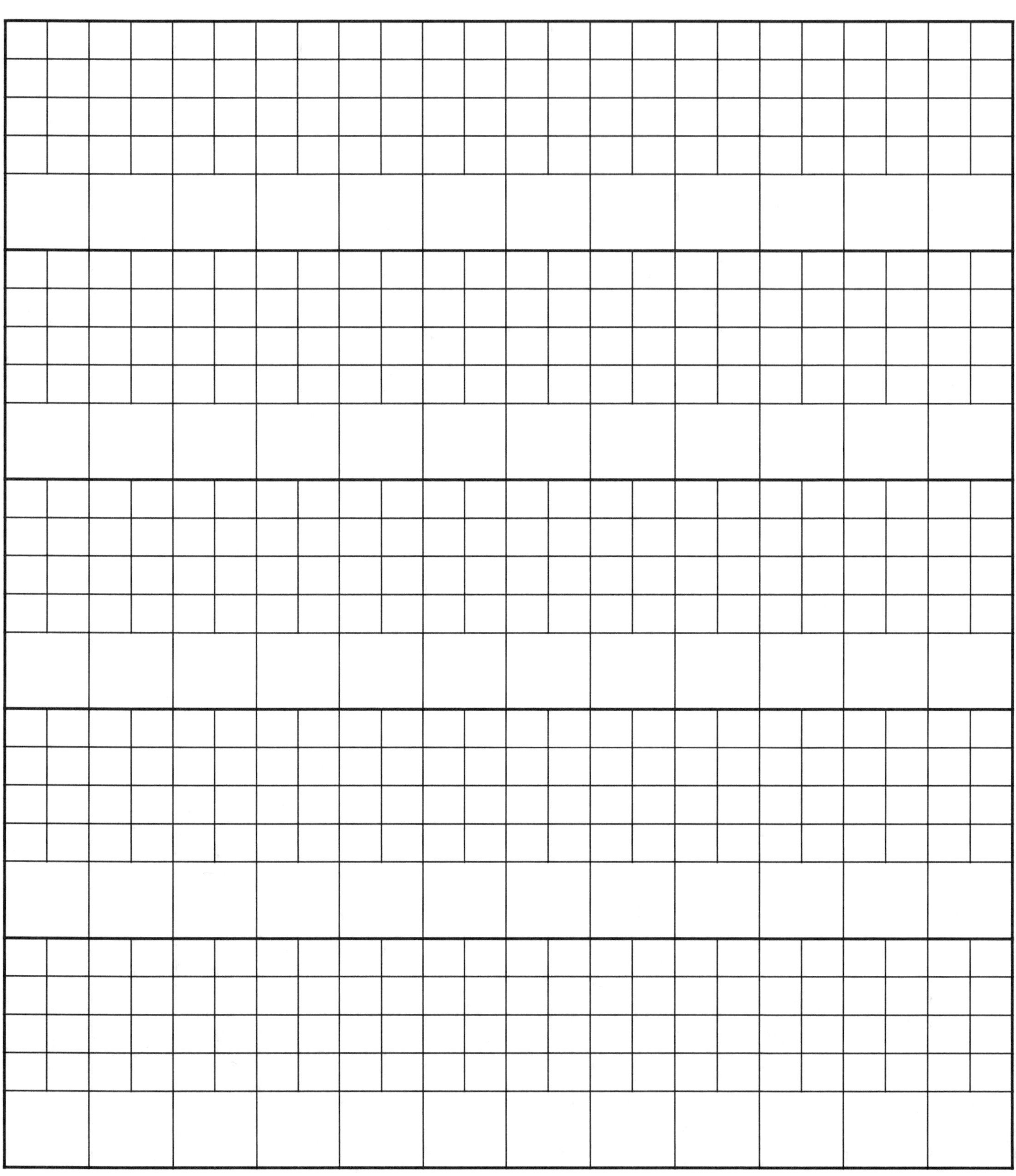

Writing Practice Sheet

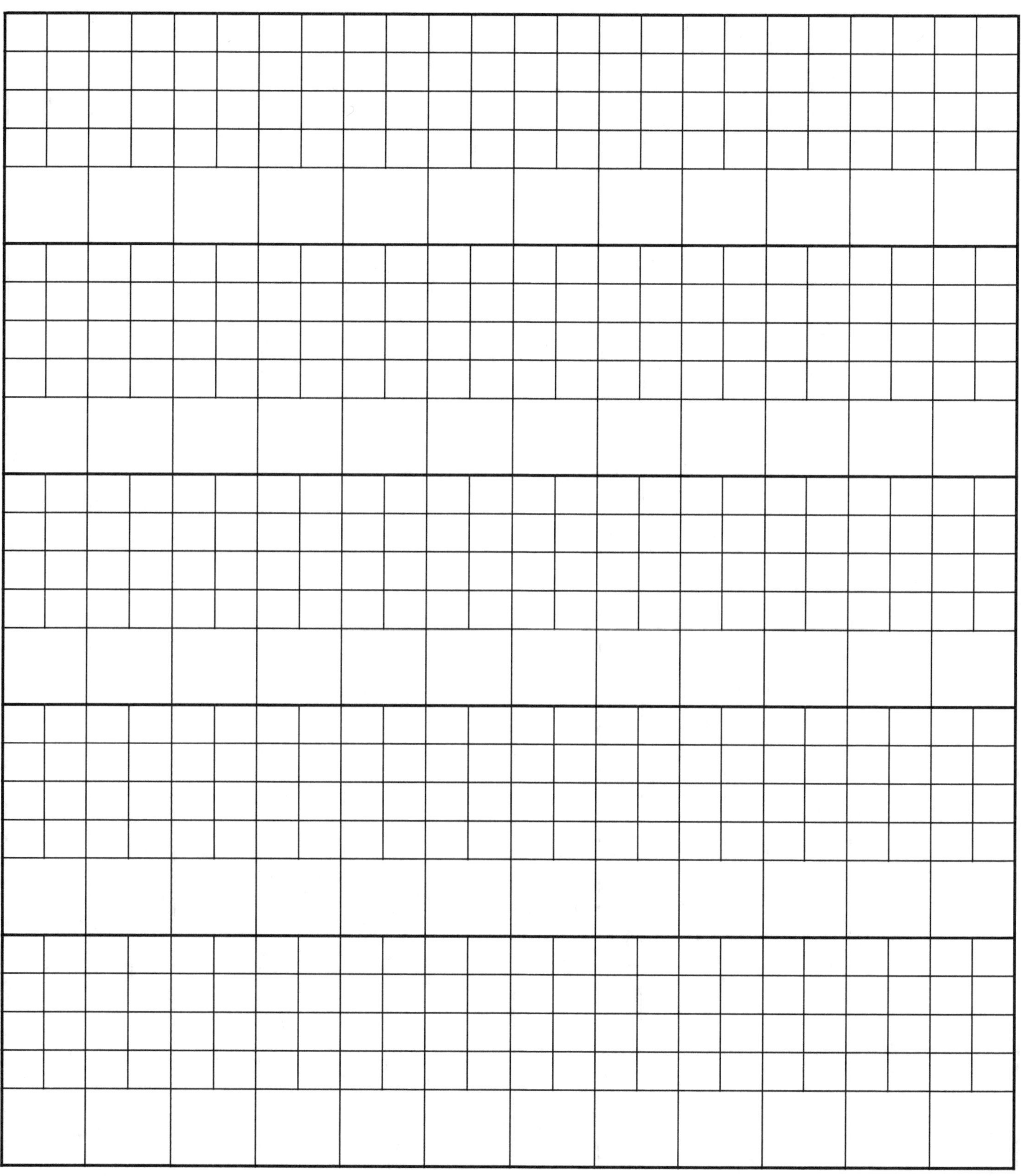

Writing Practice Sheet

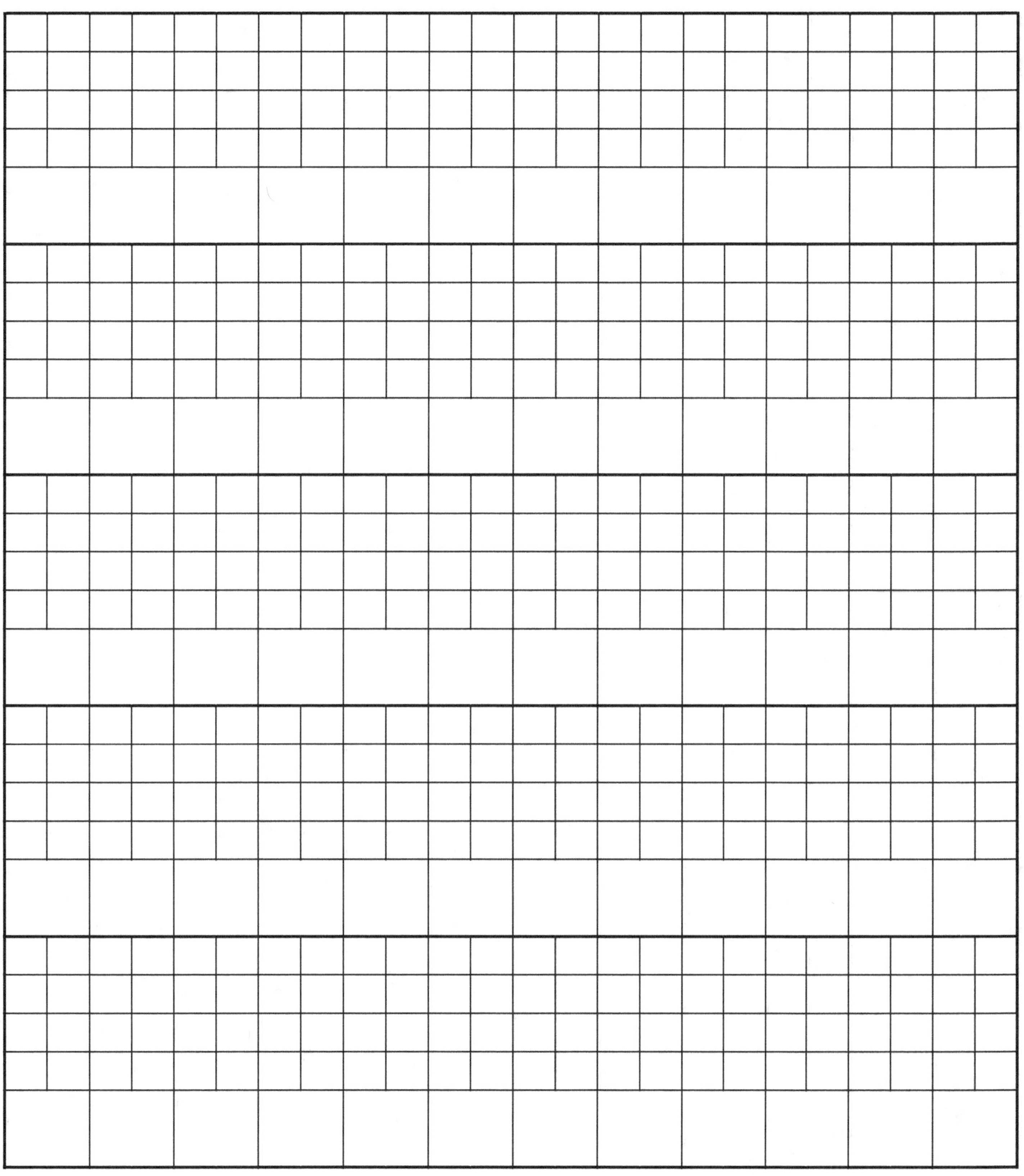

Writing Practice Sheet

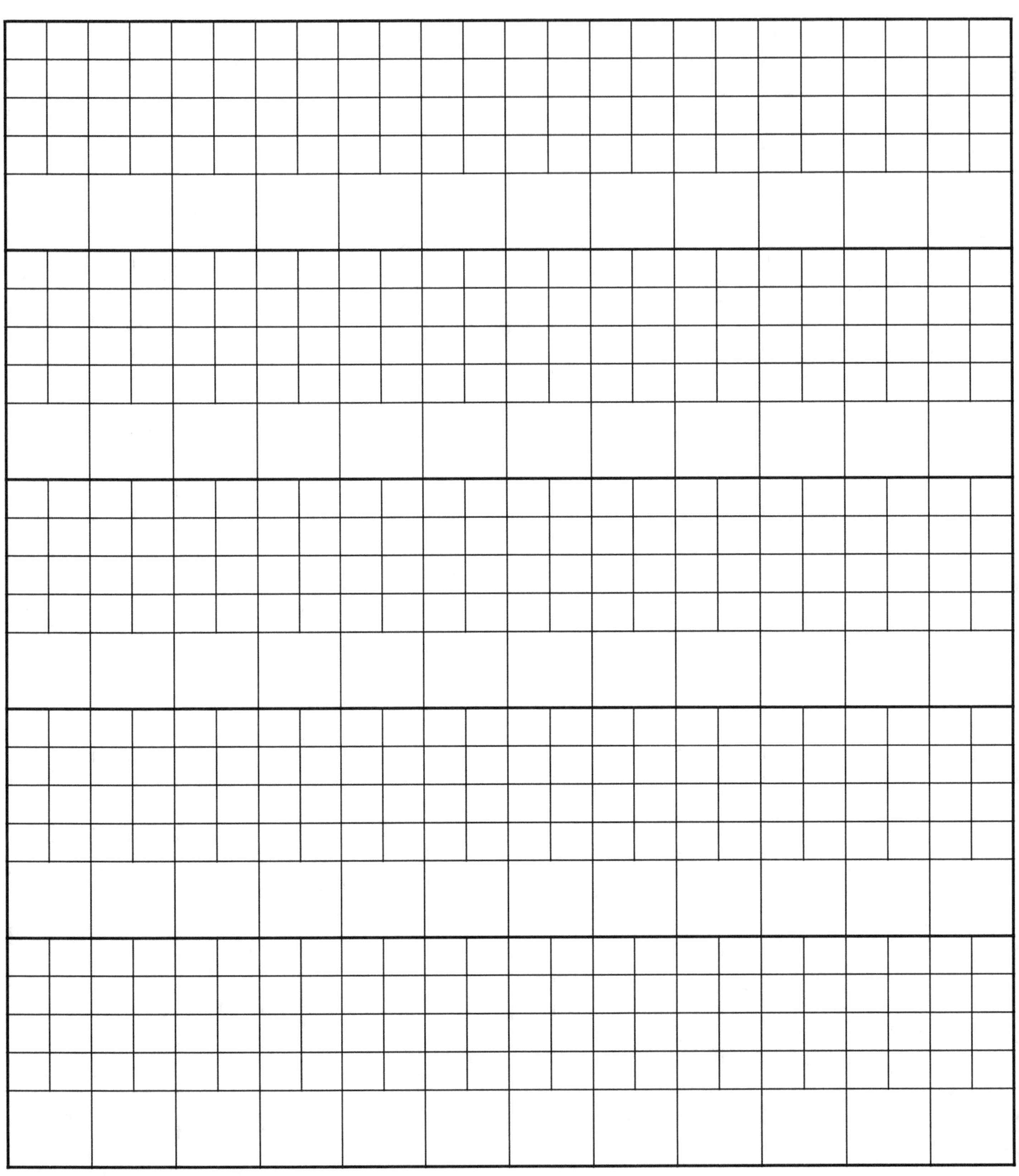

48

Writing Practice Sheet

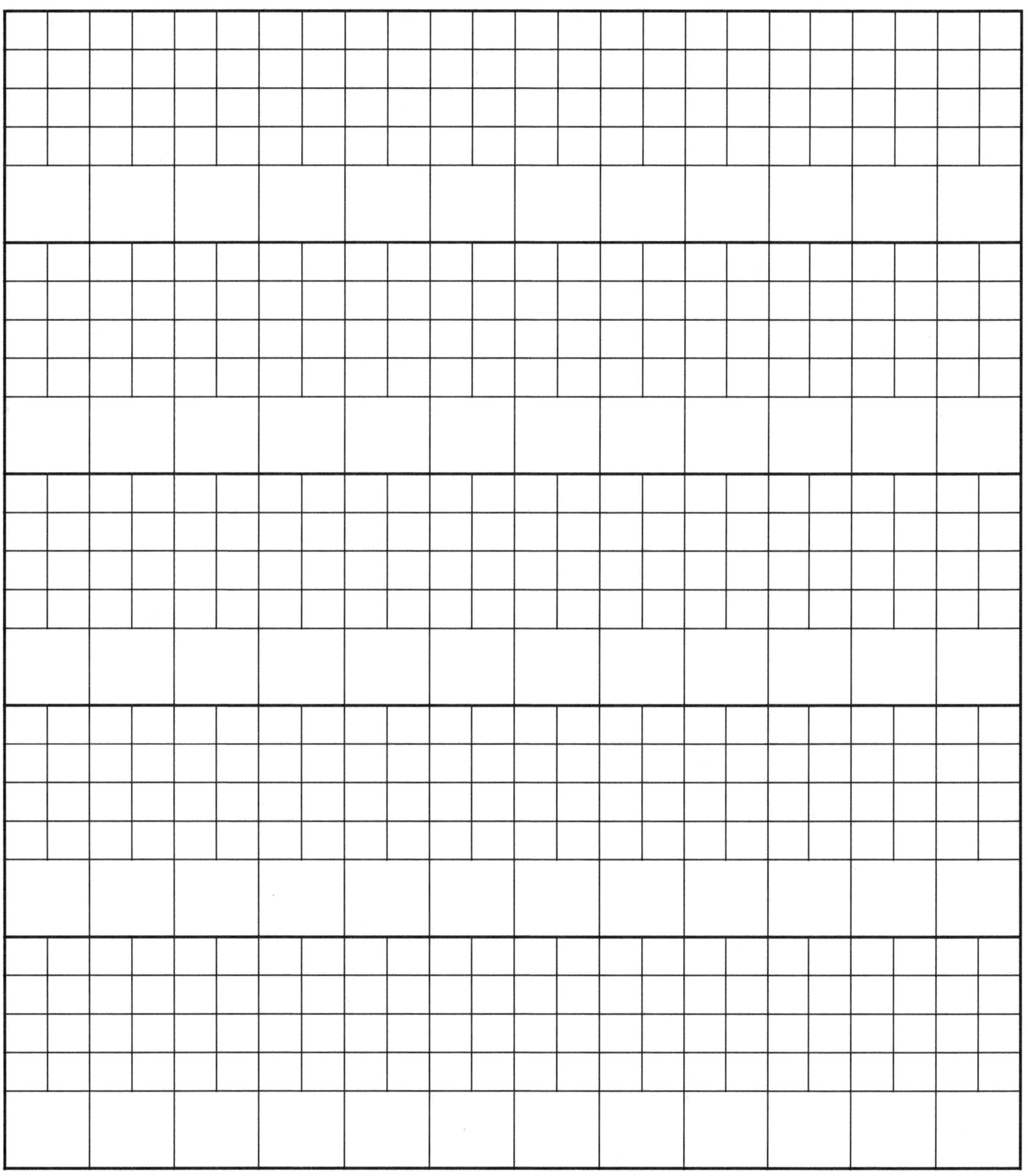

Writing Practice Sheet

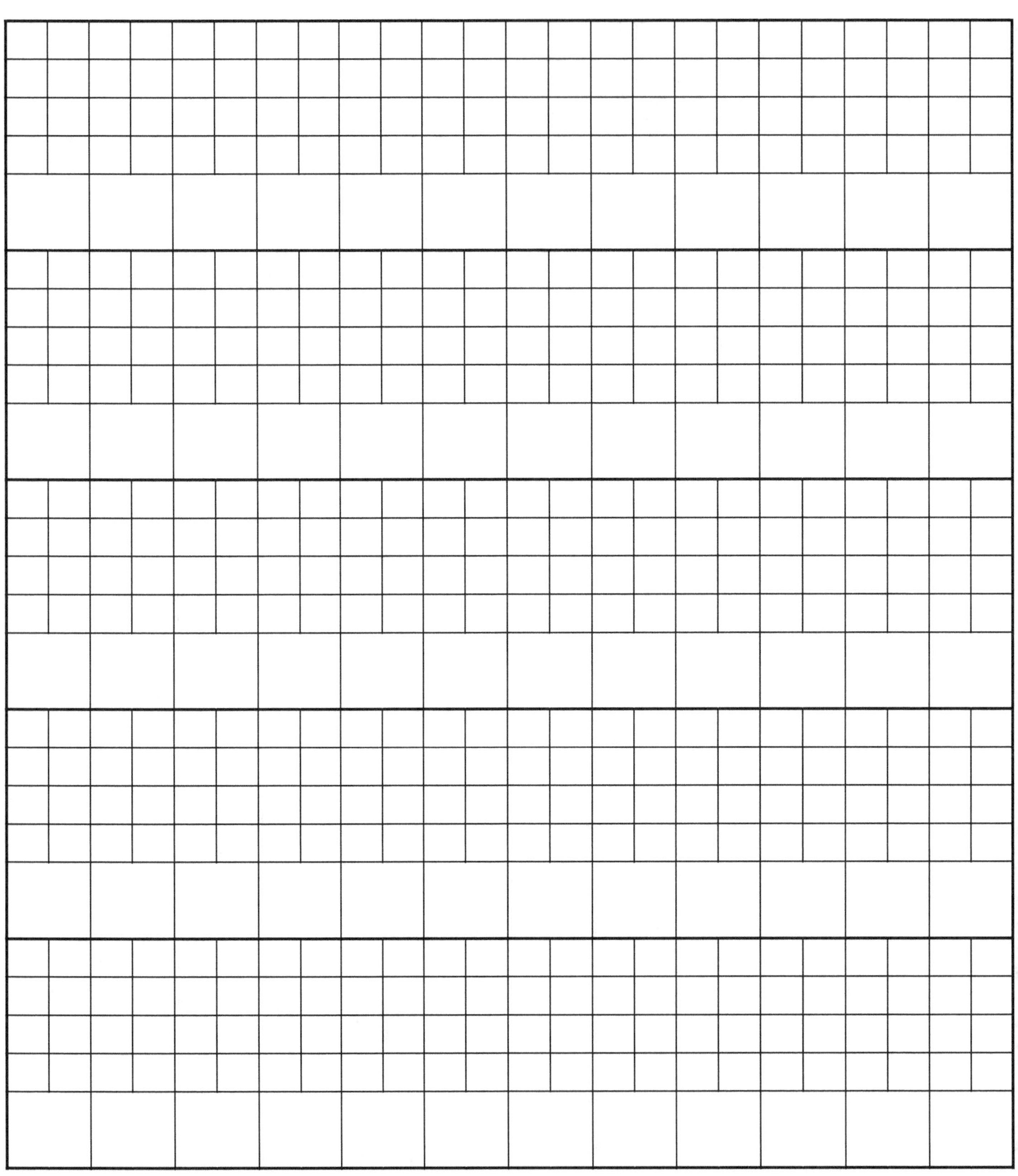

Writing Practice Sheet

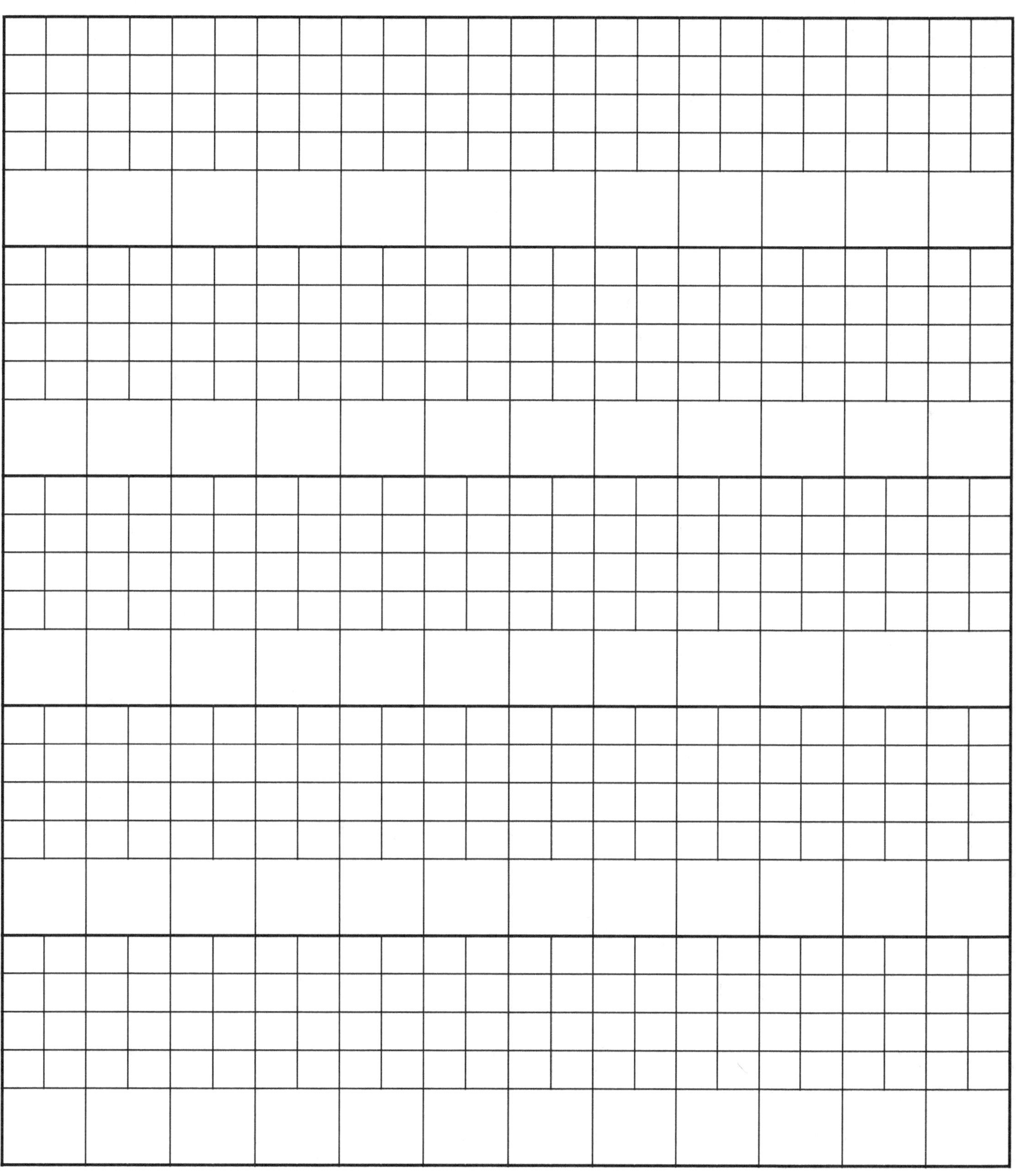

Writing Practice Sheet

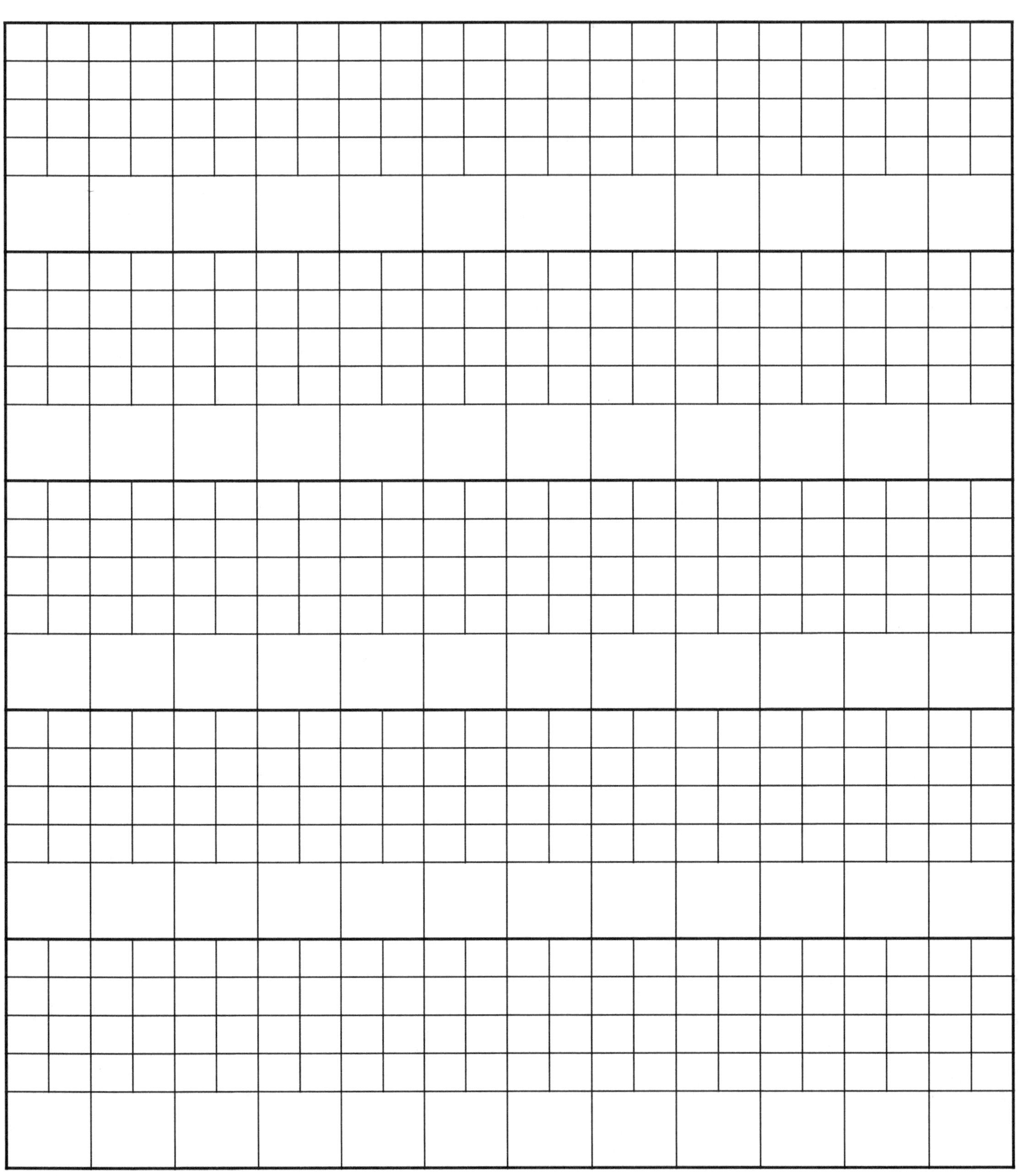

Writing Practice Sheet

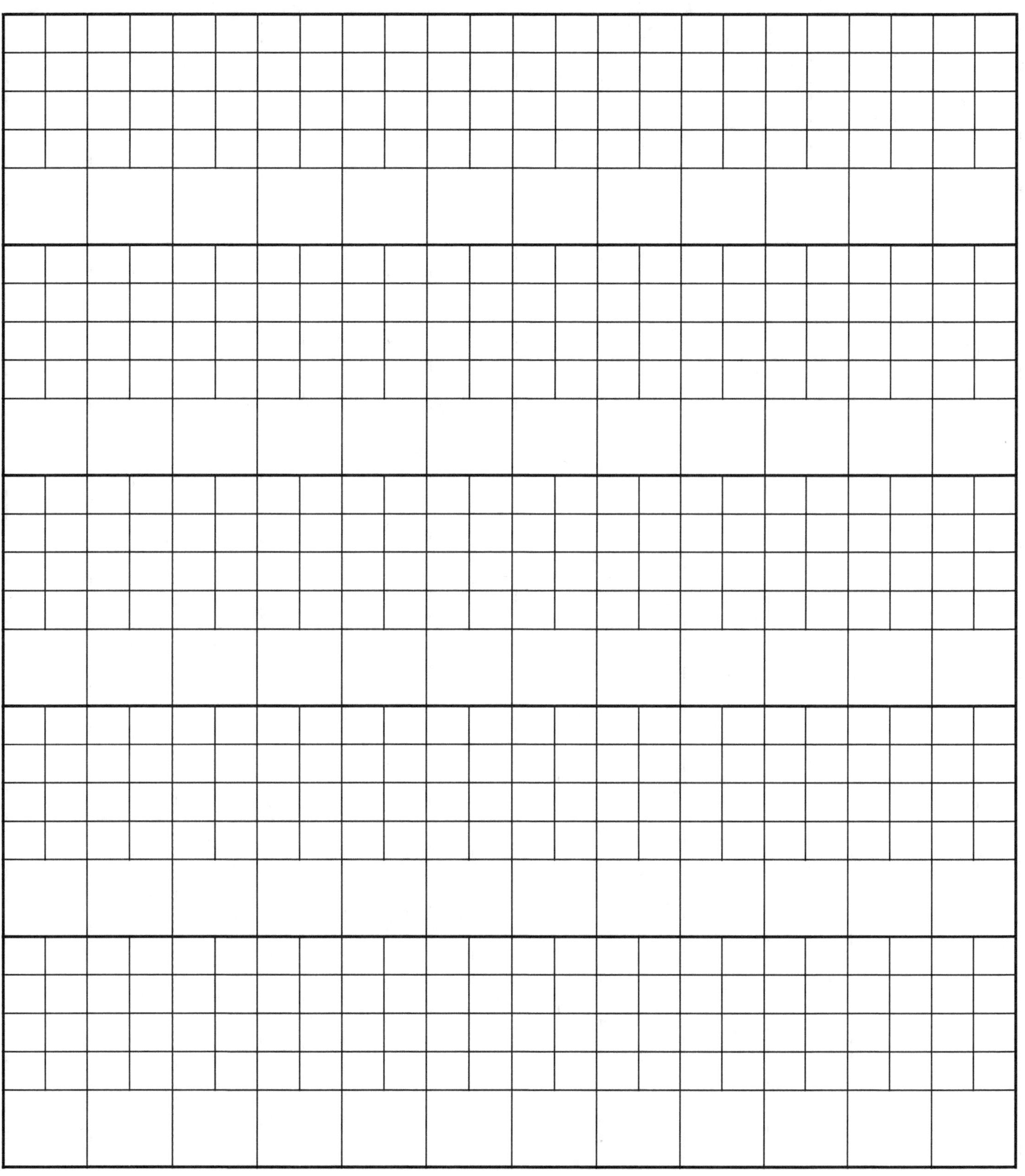

Writing Practice Sheet

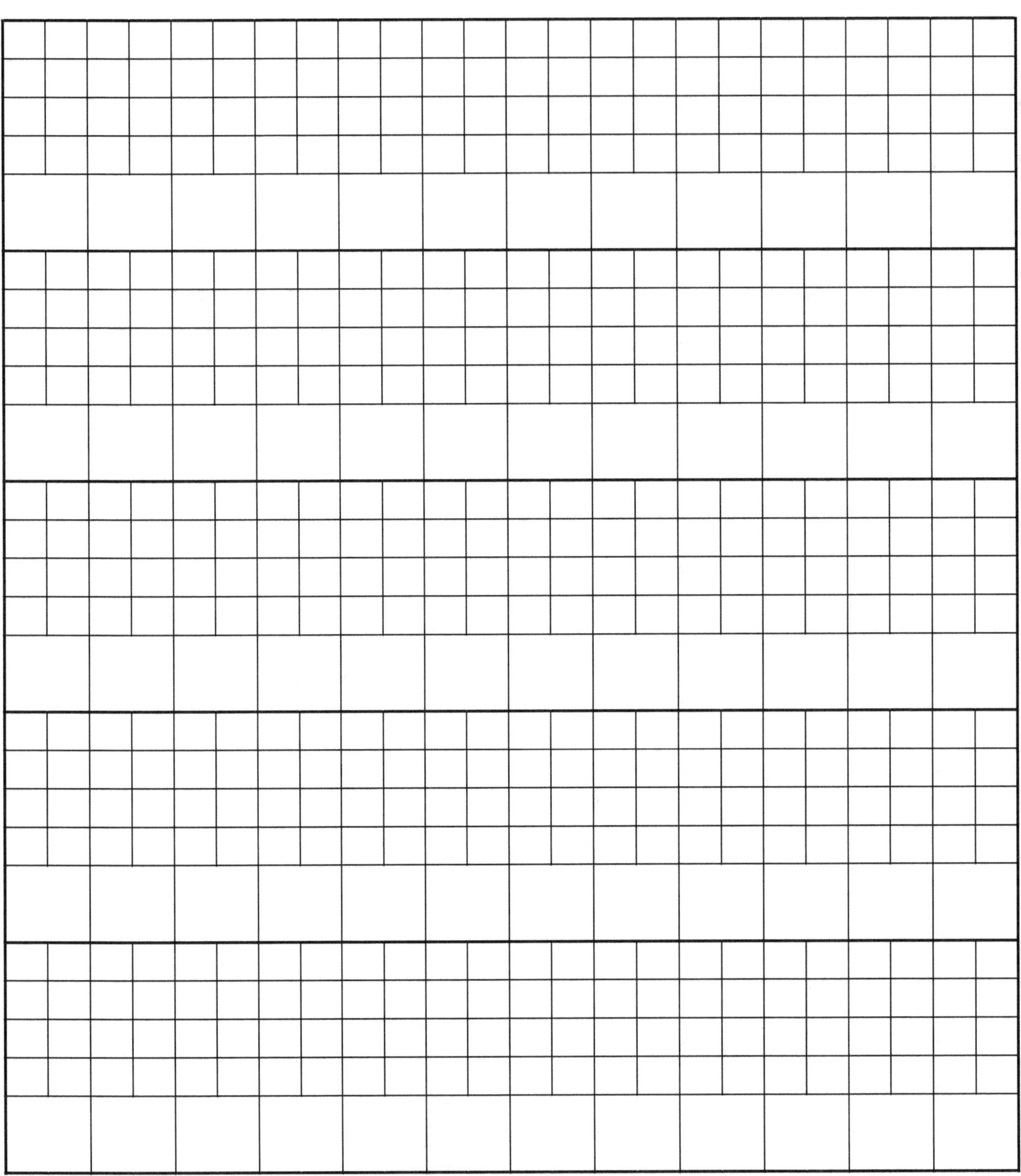

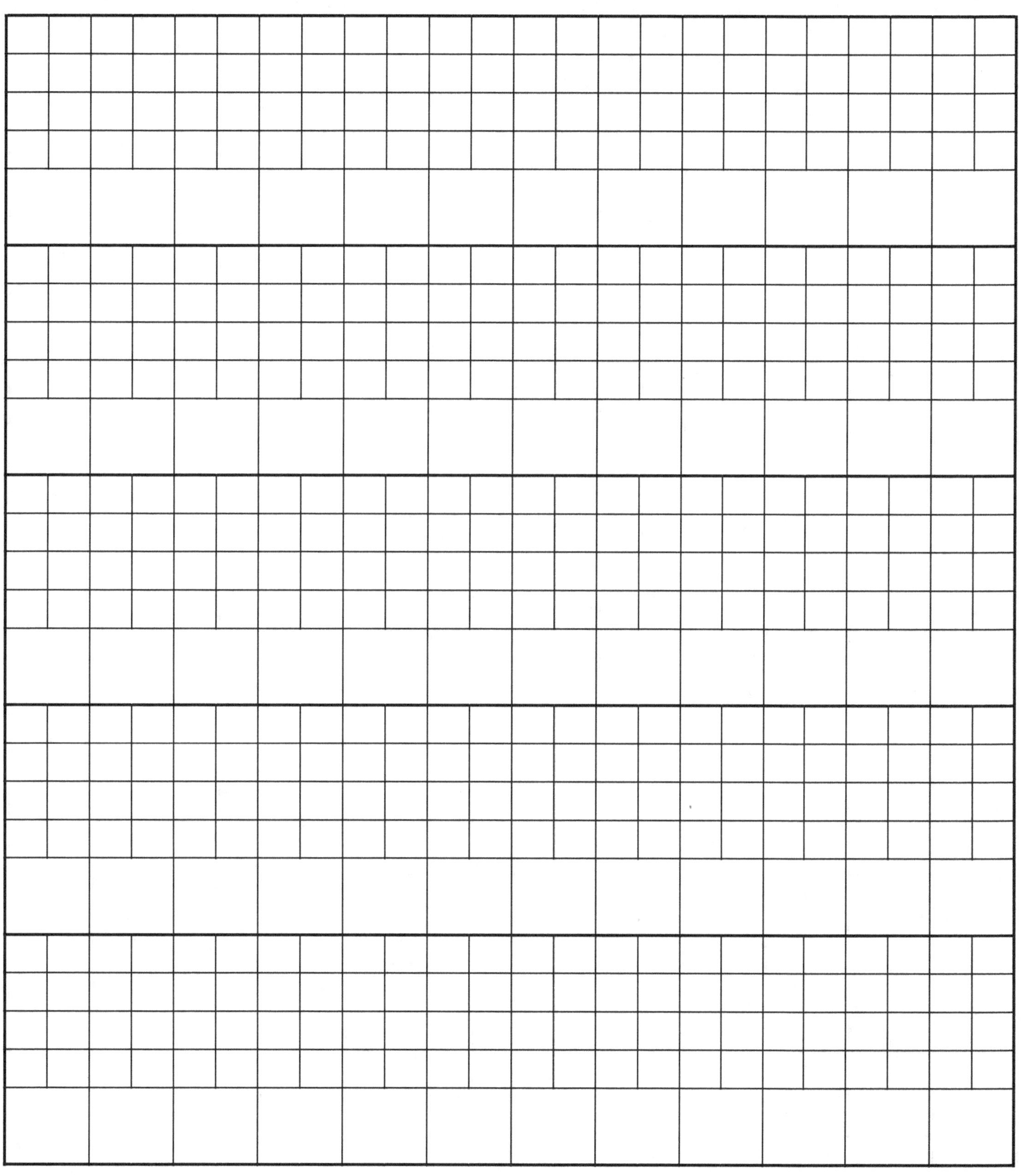

Writing Practice Sheet

Writing Practice Sheet

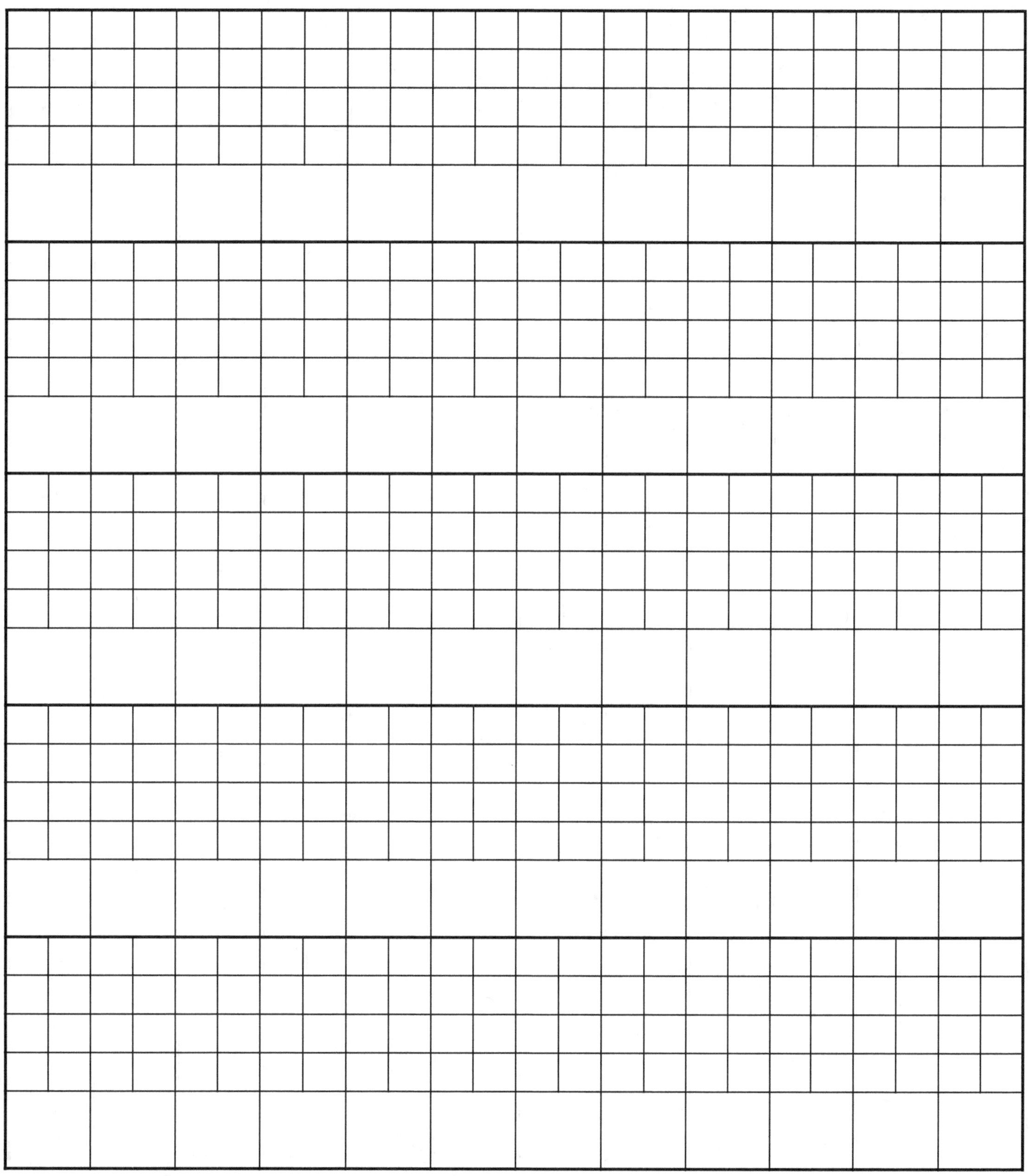

Writing Practice Sheet

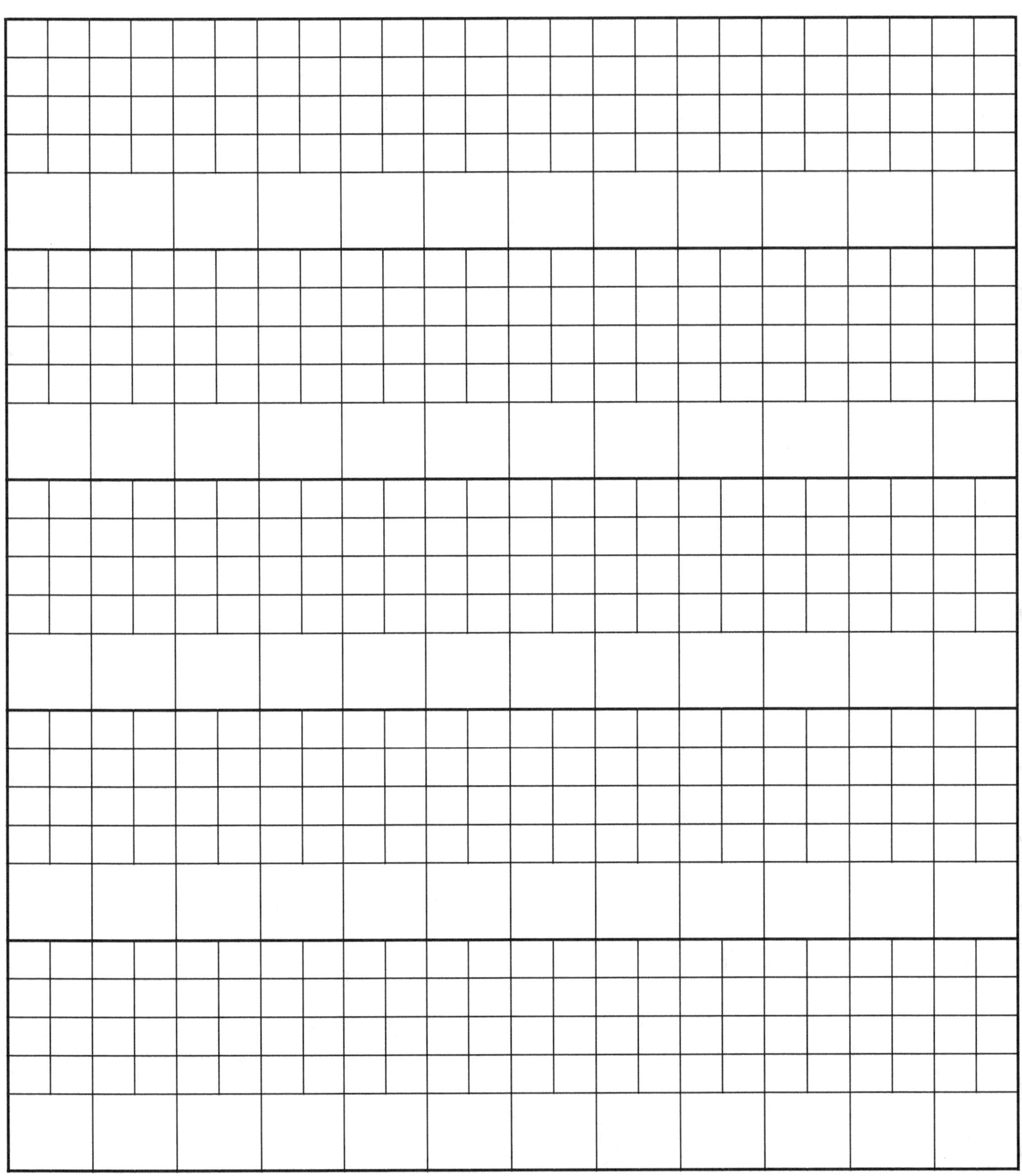

Writing Practice Sheet

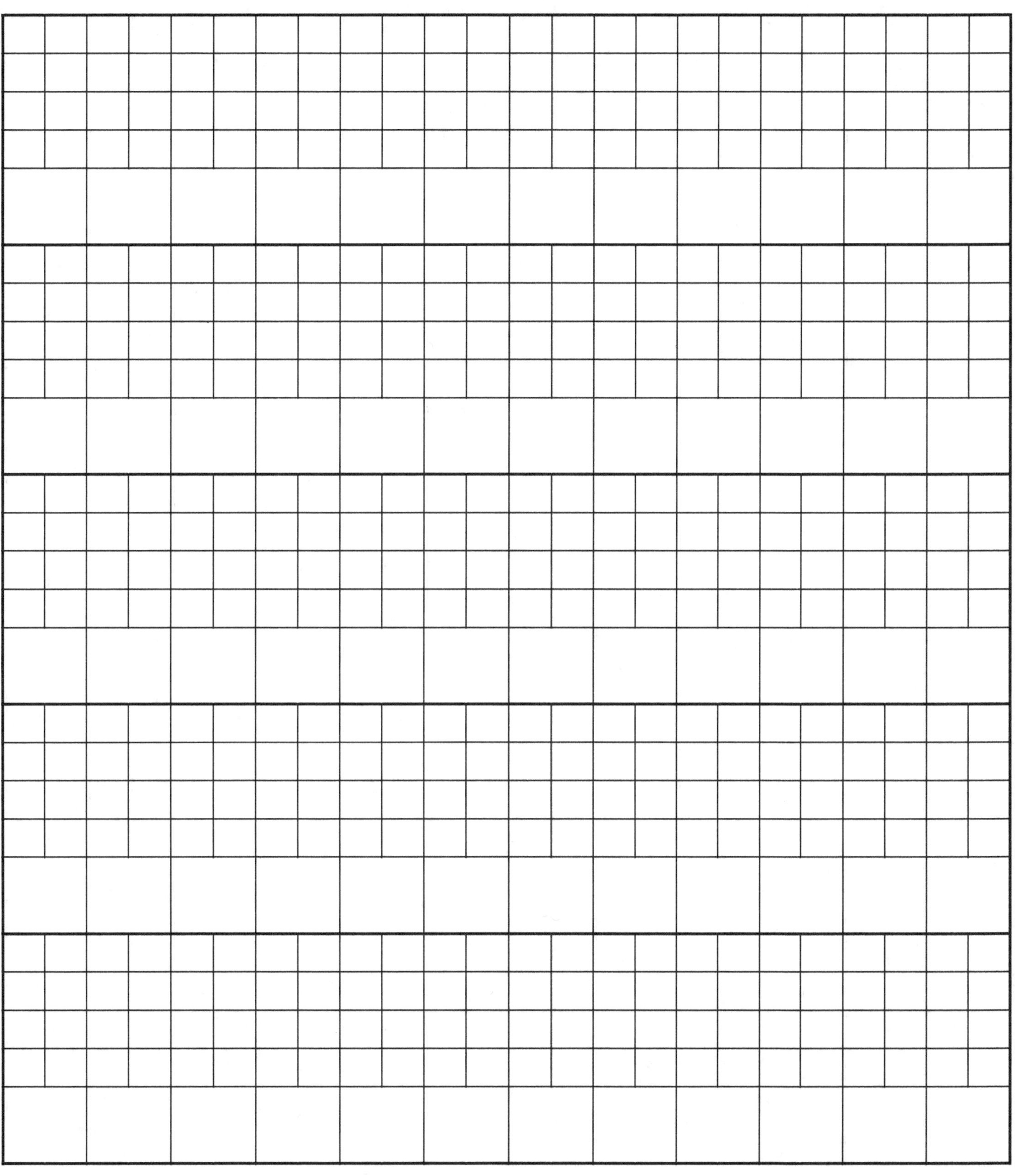

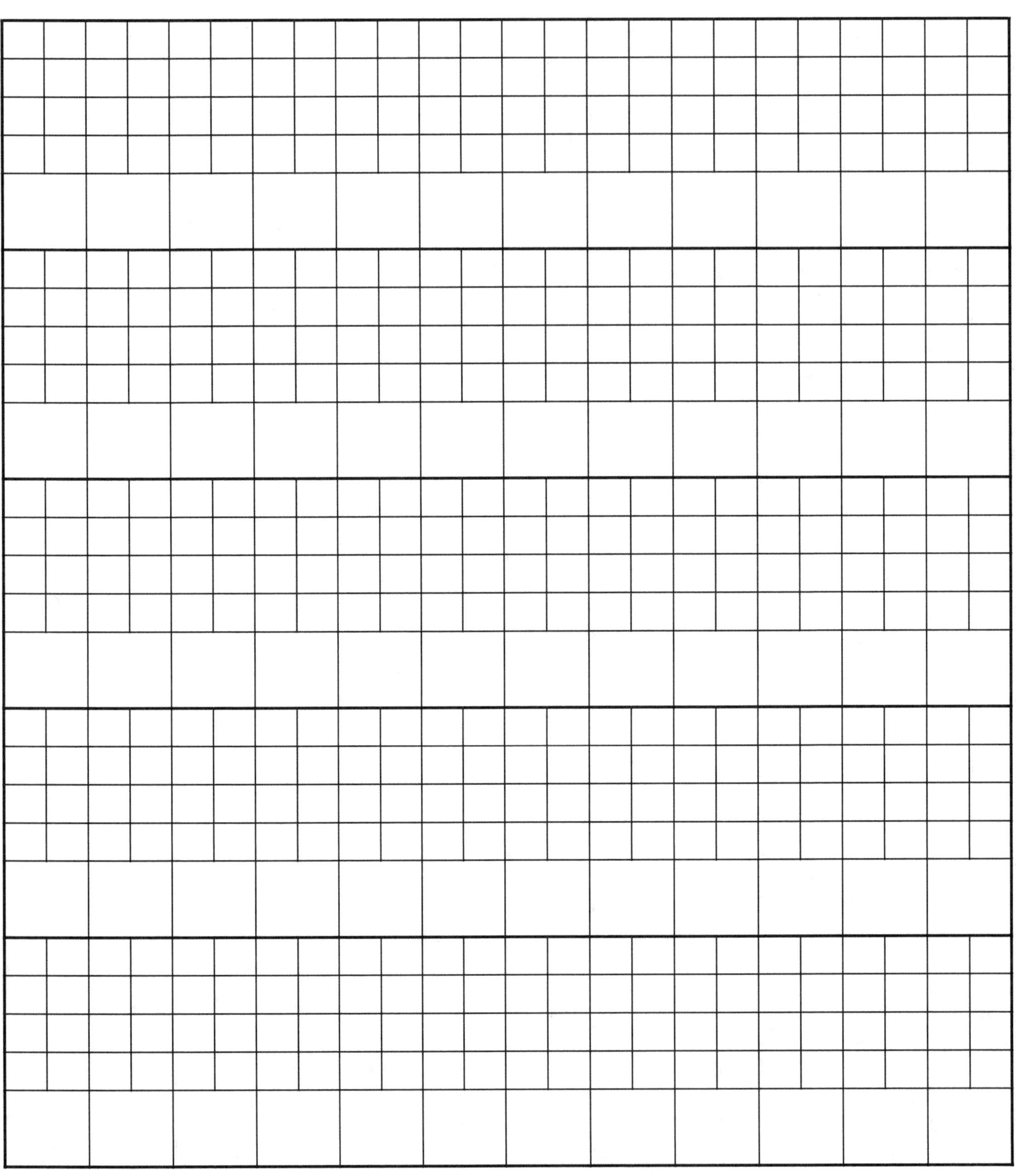

Writing Practice Sheet

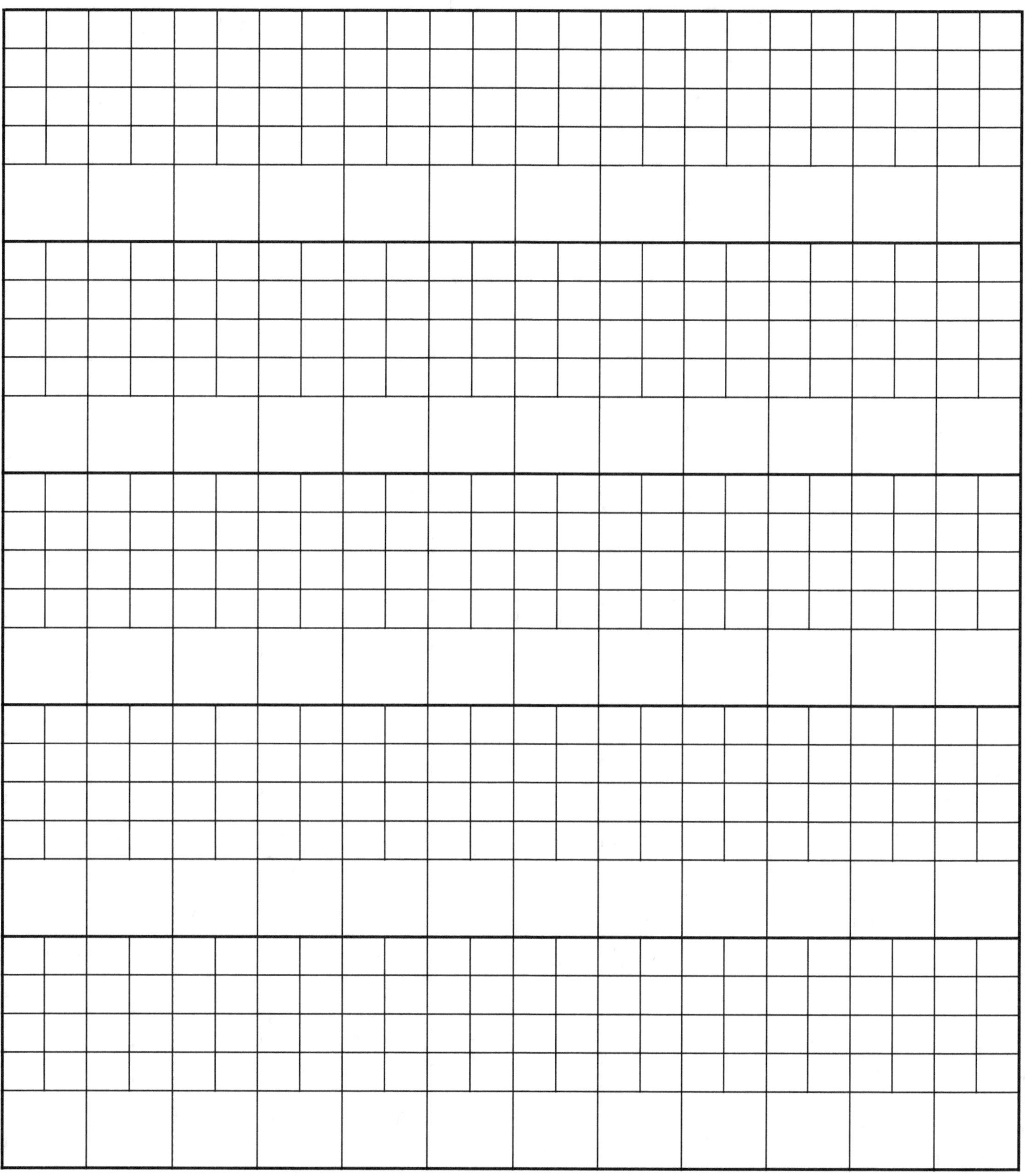

Writing Practice Sheet

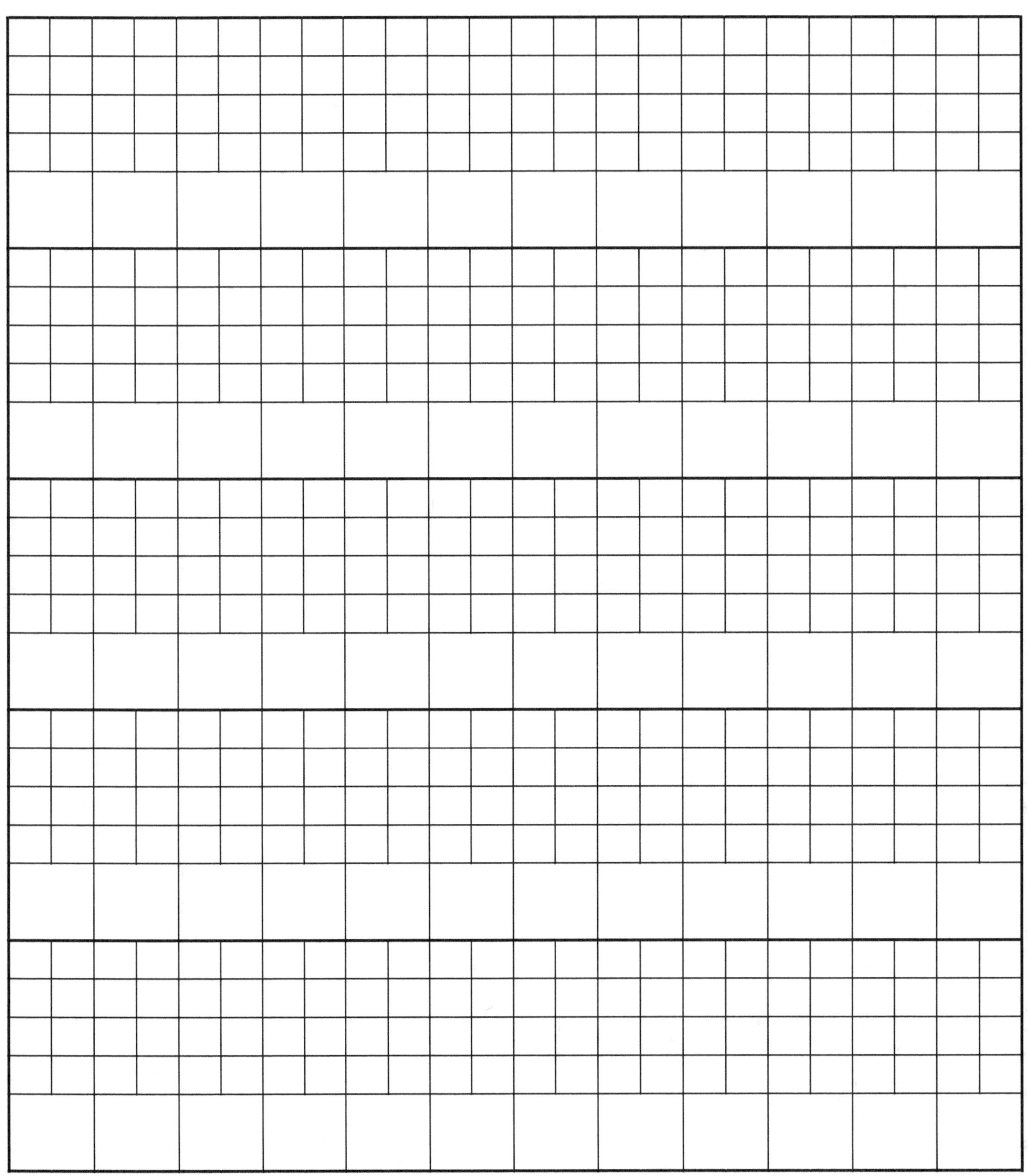

Writing Practice Sheet

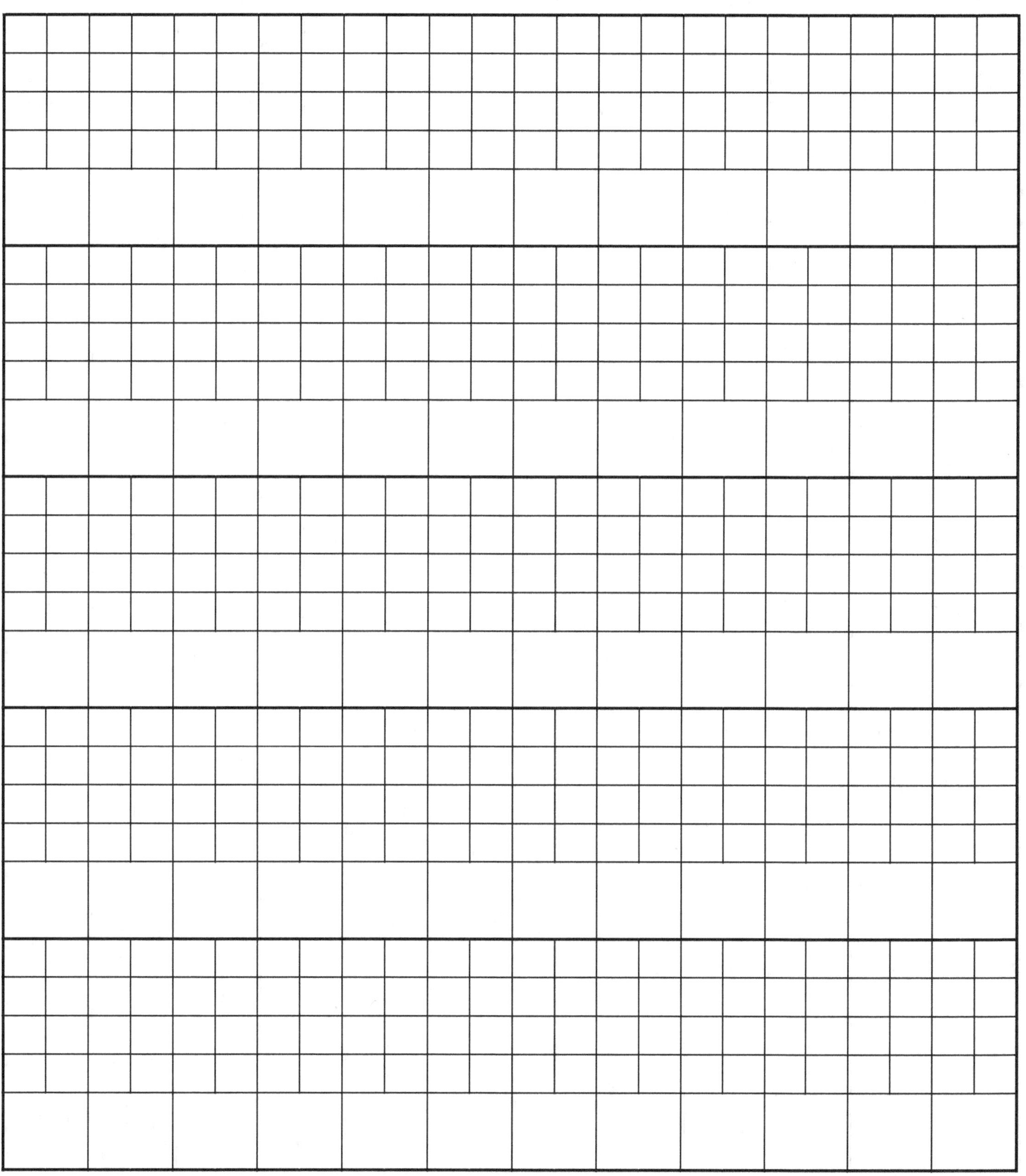

Writing Practice Sheet

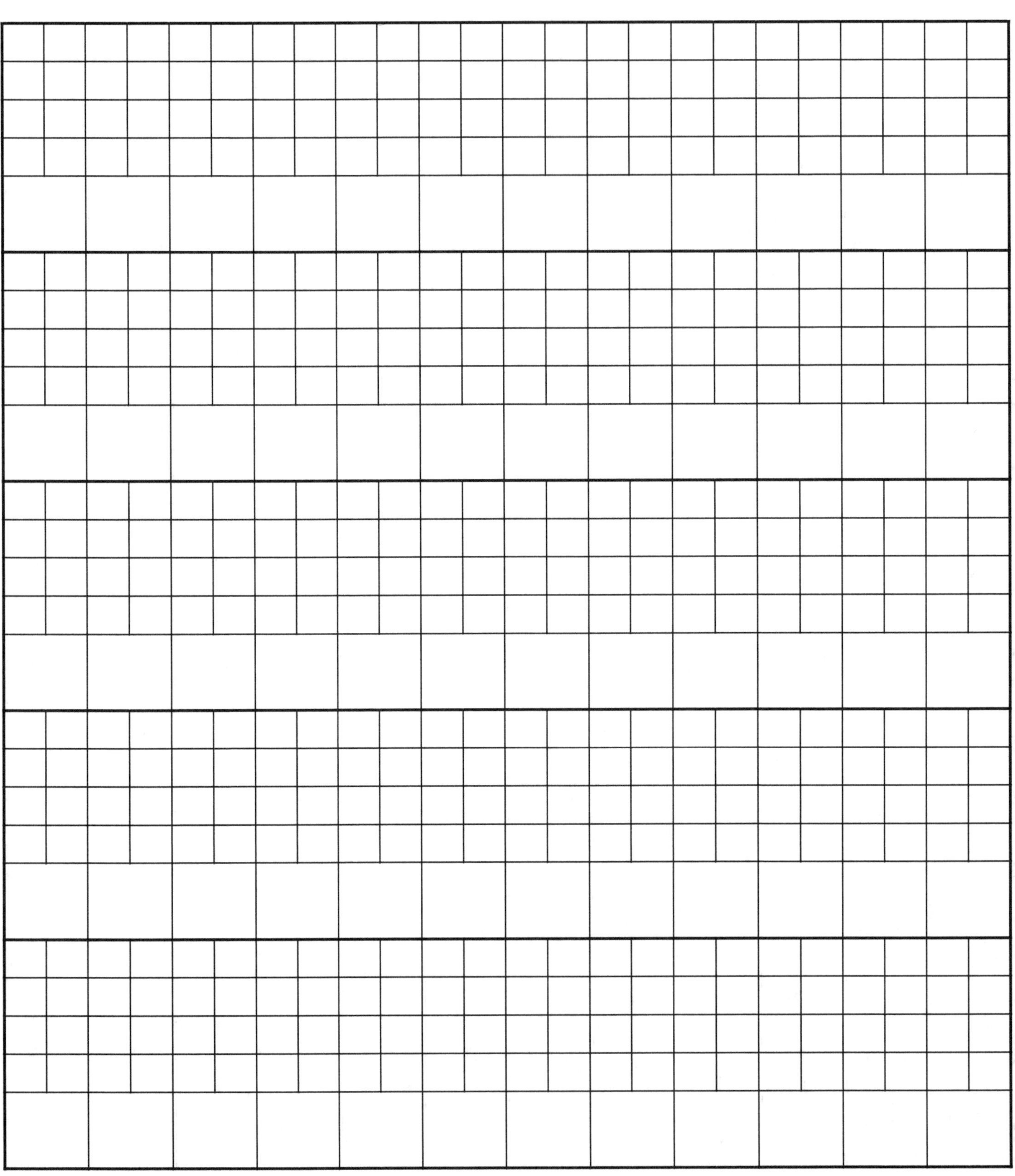

Writing Practice Sheet

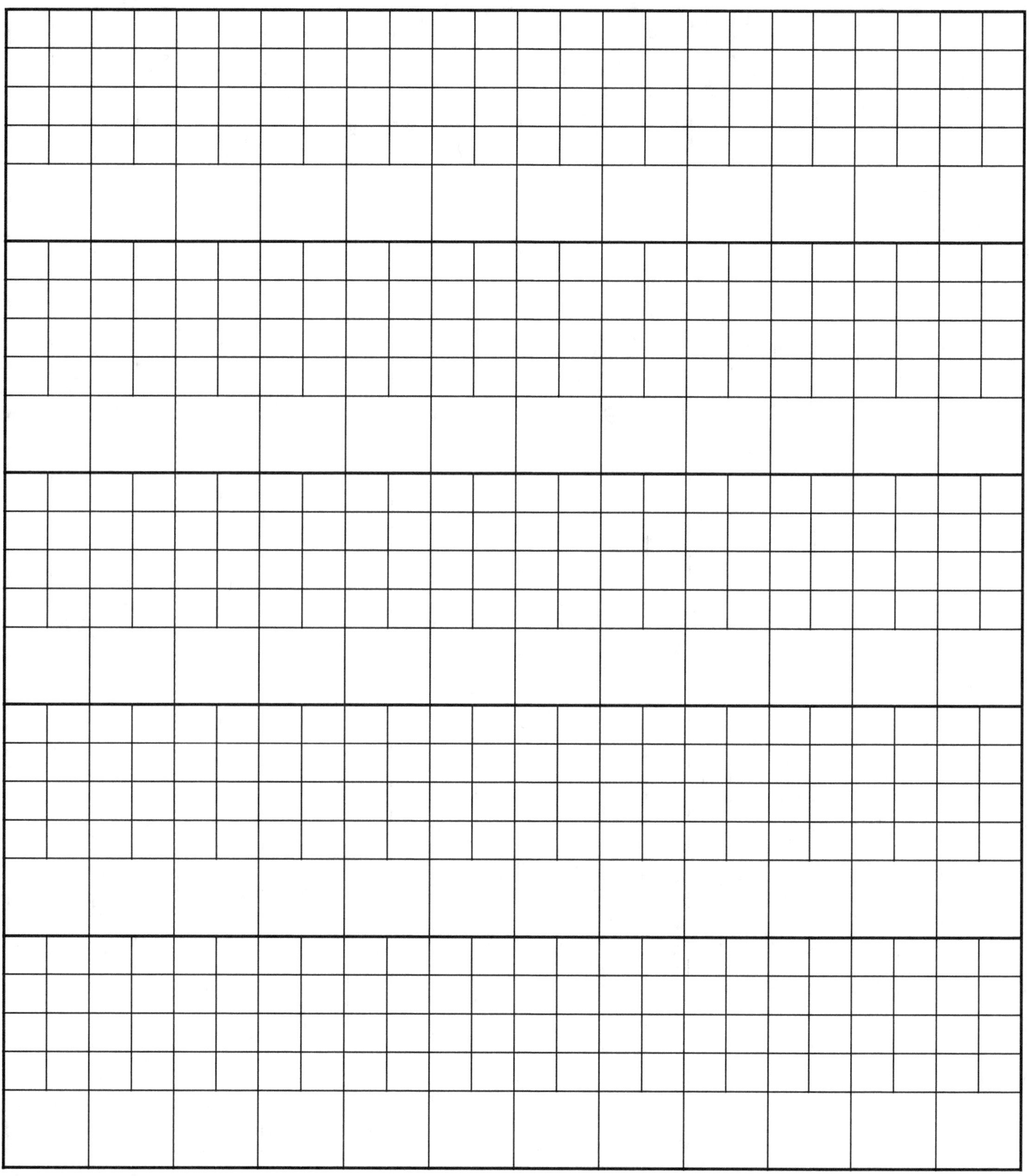

Writing Practice Sheet

Writing Practice Sheet

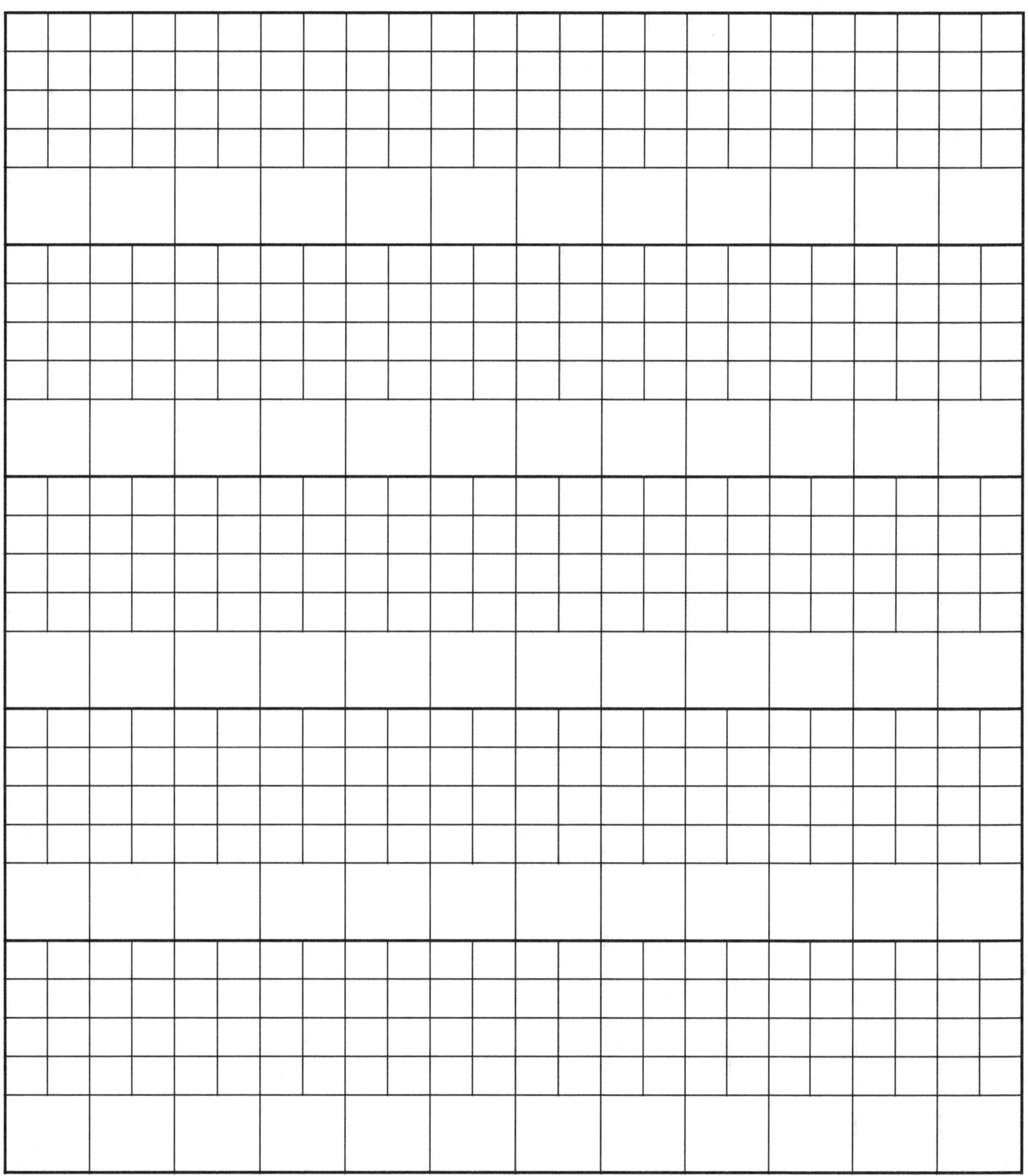

Writing Practice Sheet

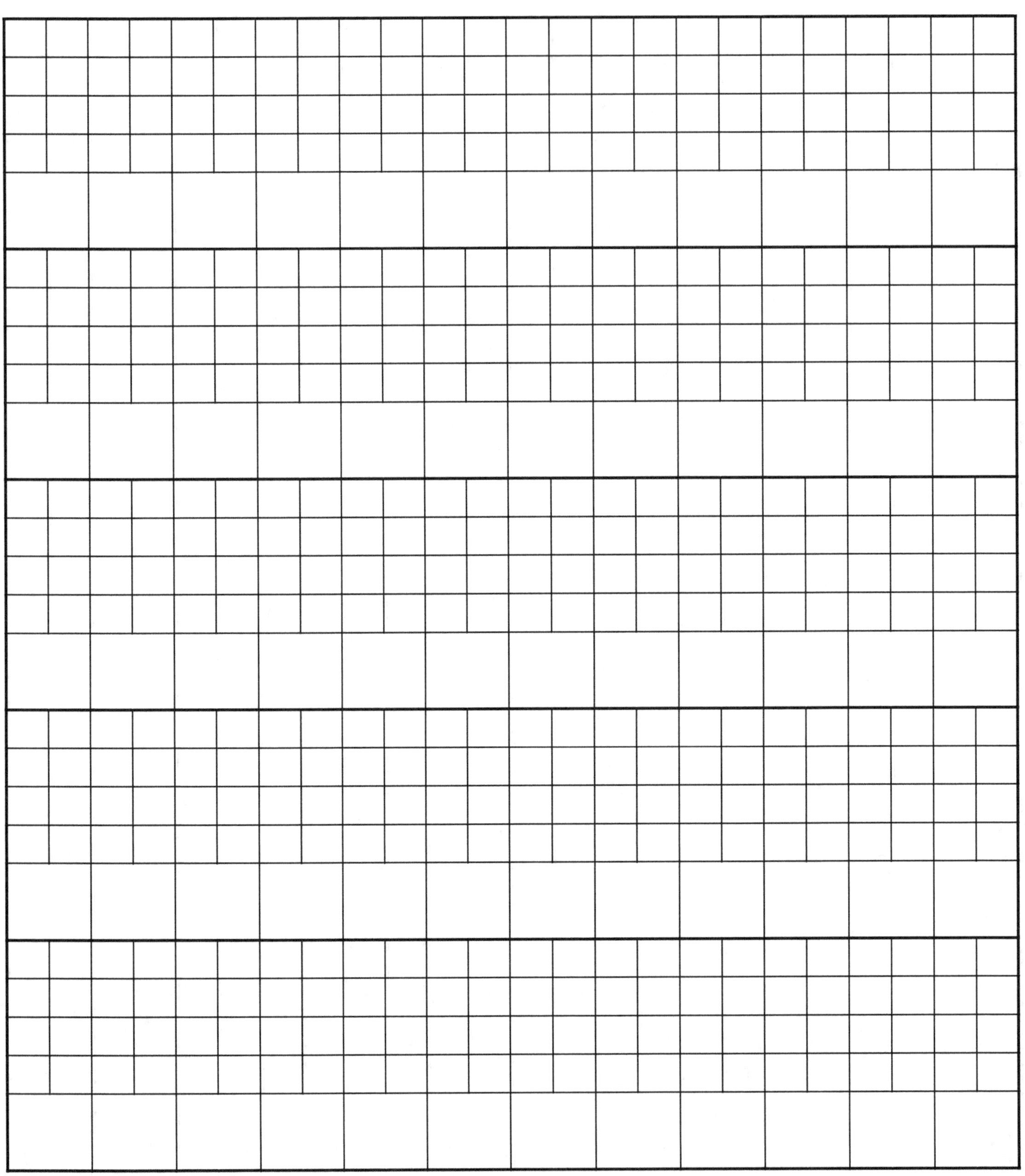

Writing Practice Sheet

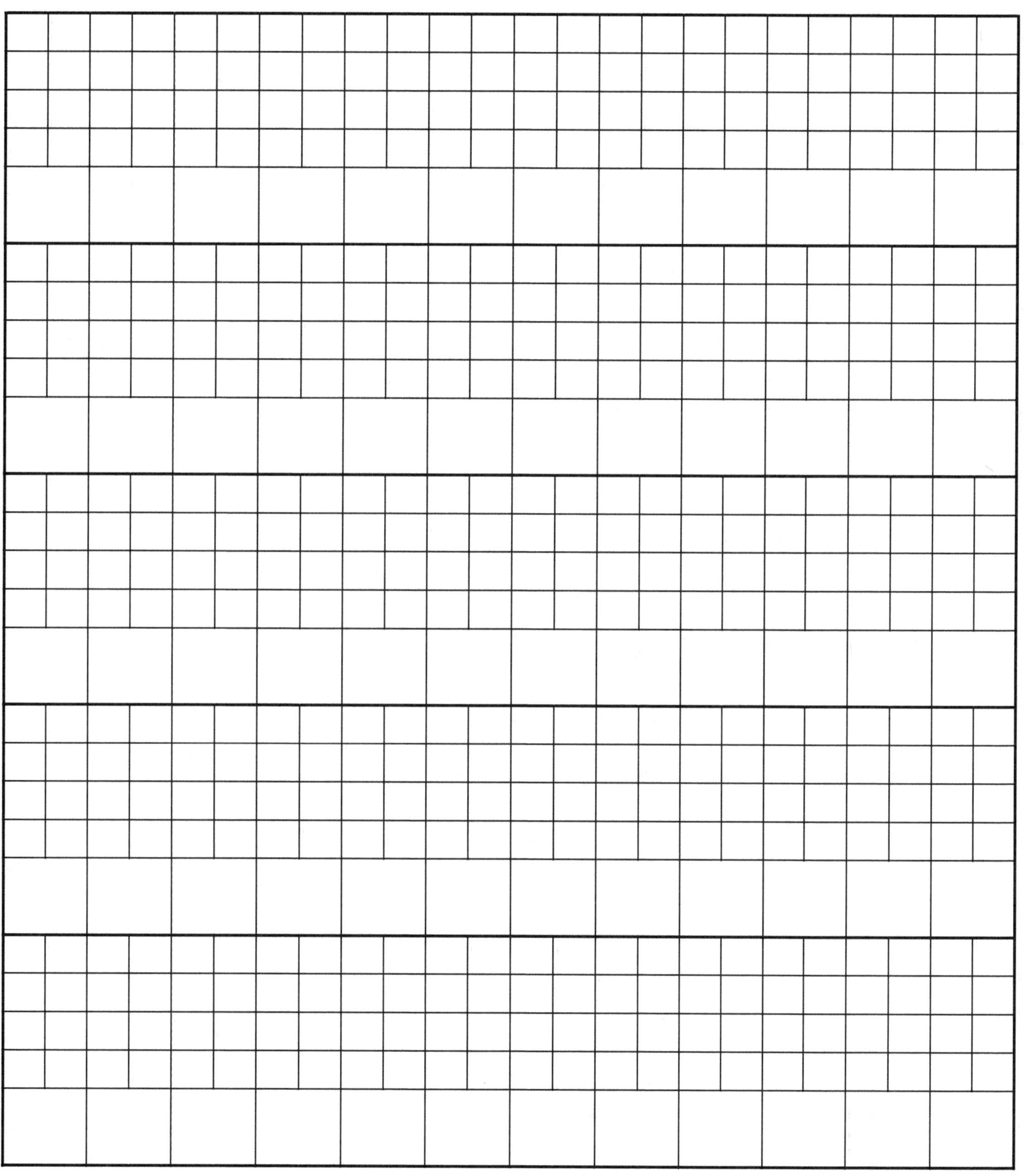

Writing Practice Sheet

Writing Practice Sheet

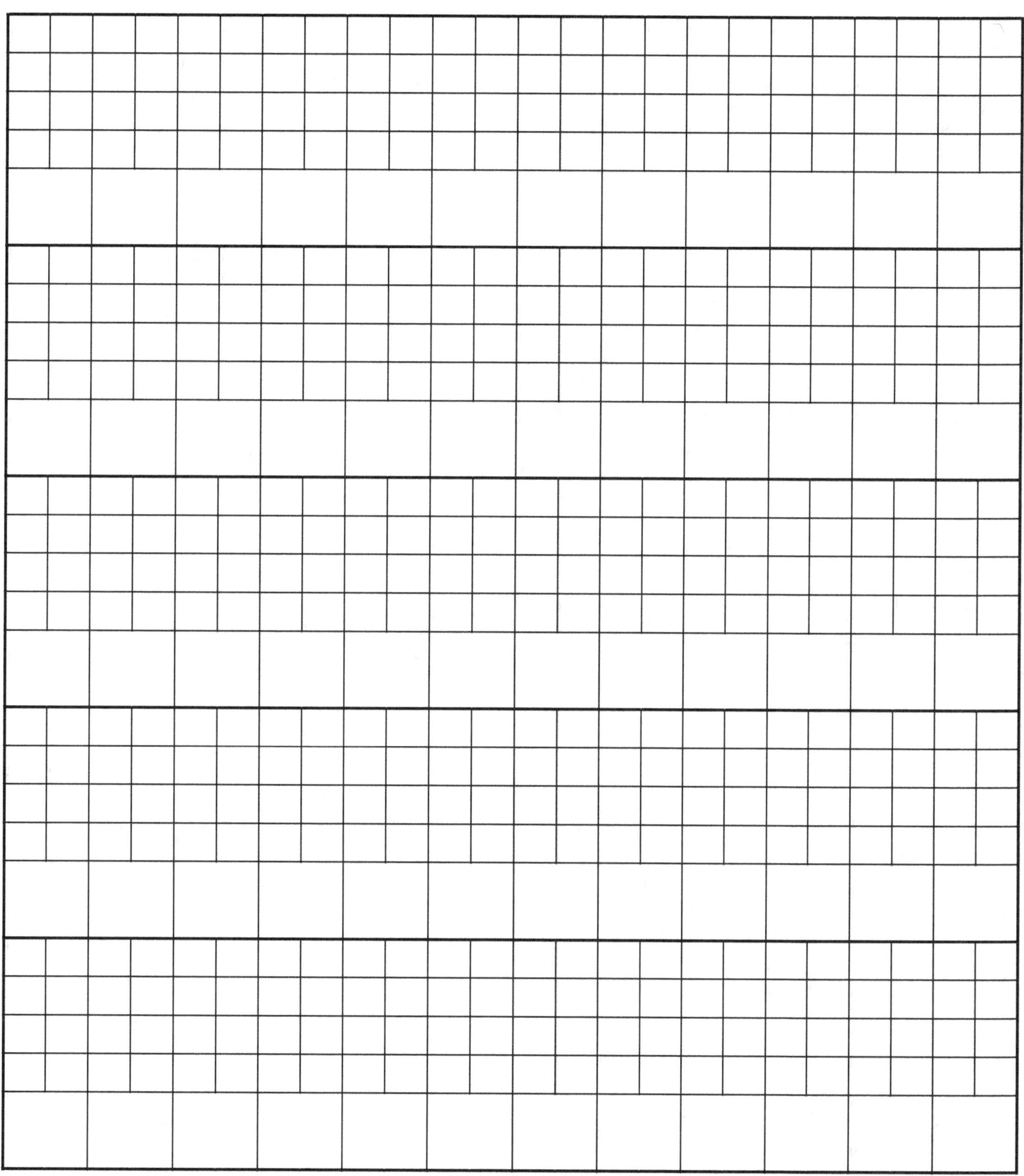

Writing Practice Sheet

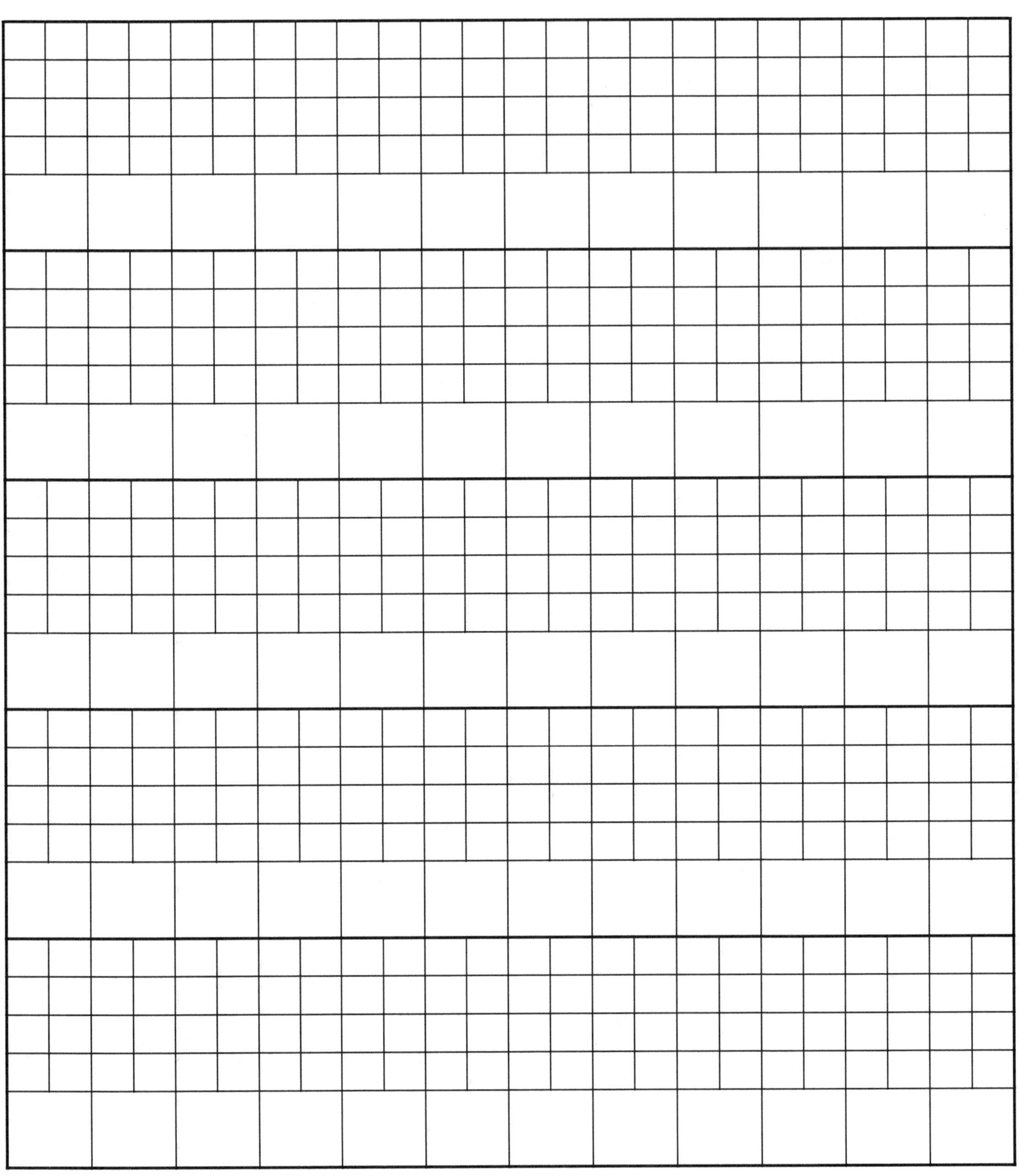

Writing Practice Sheet

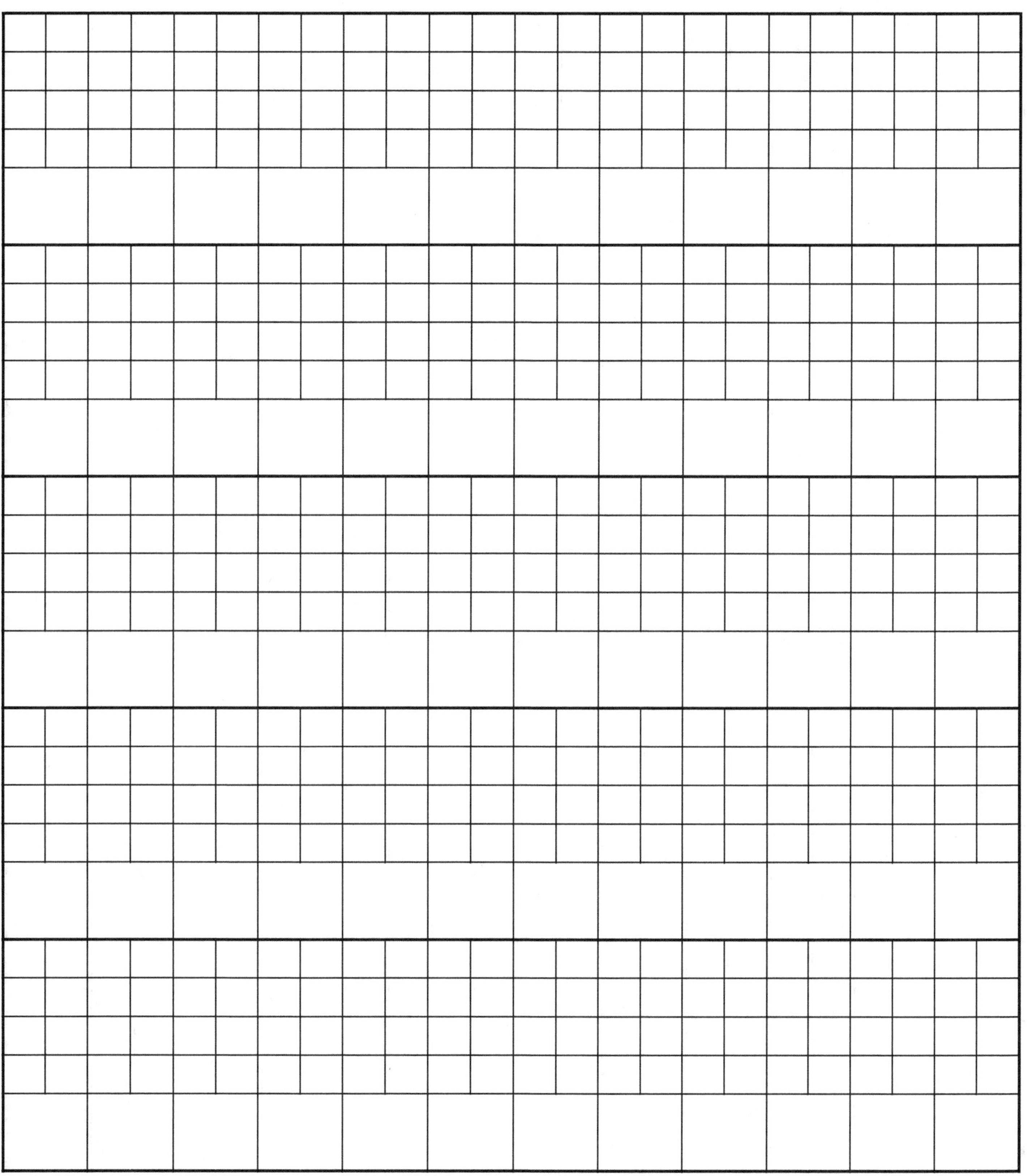

Writing Practice Sheet

Writing Practice Sheet

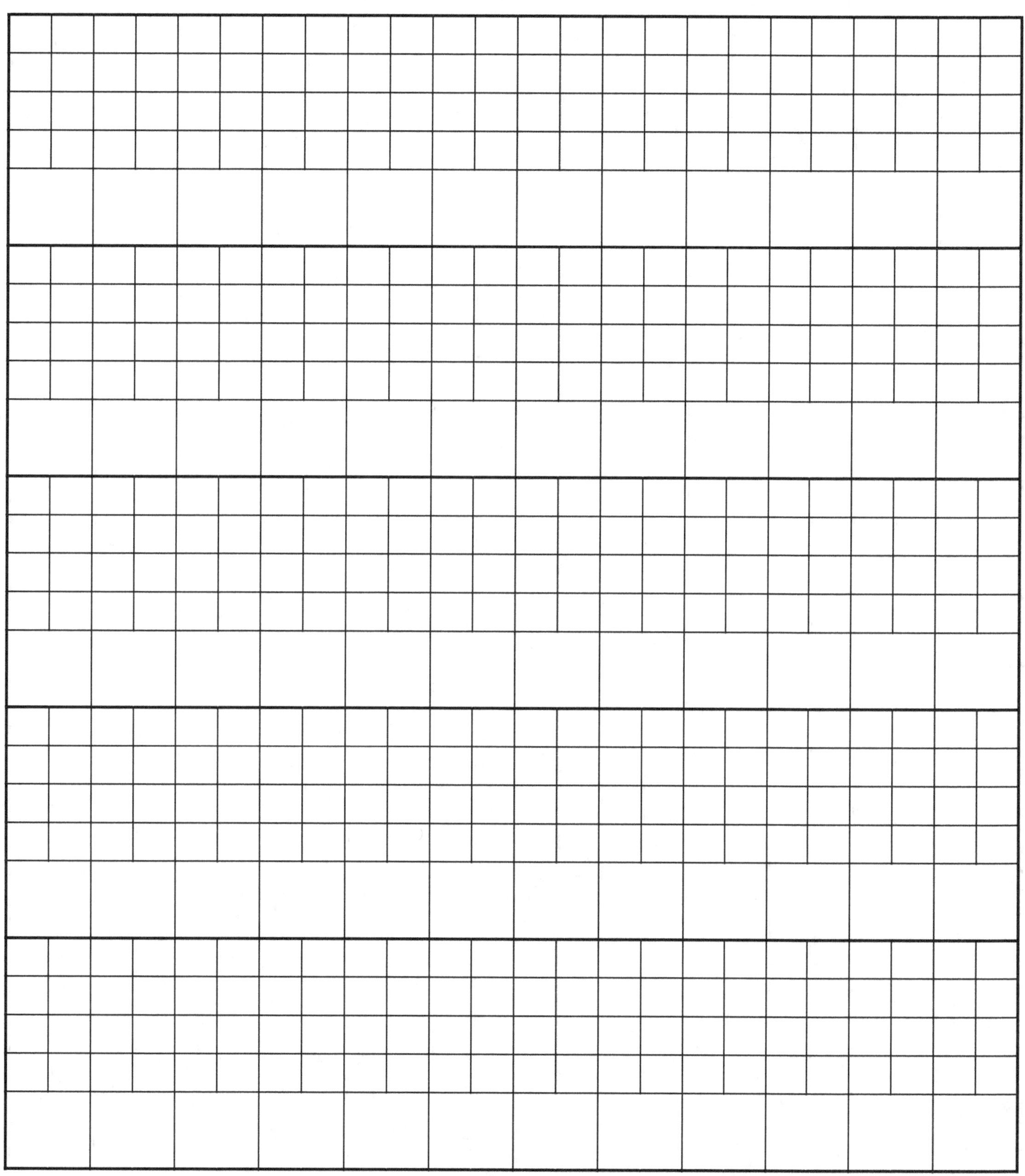

Writing Practice Sheet

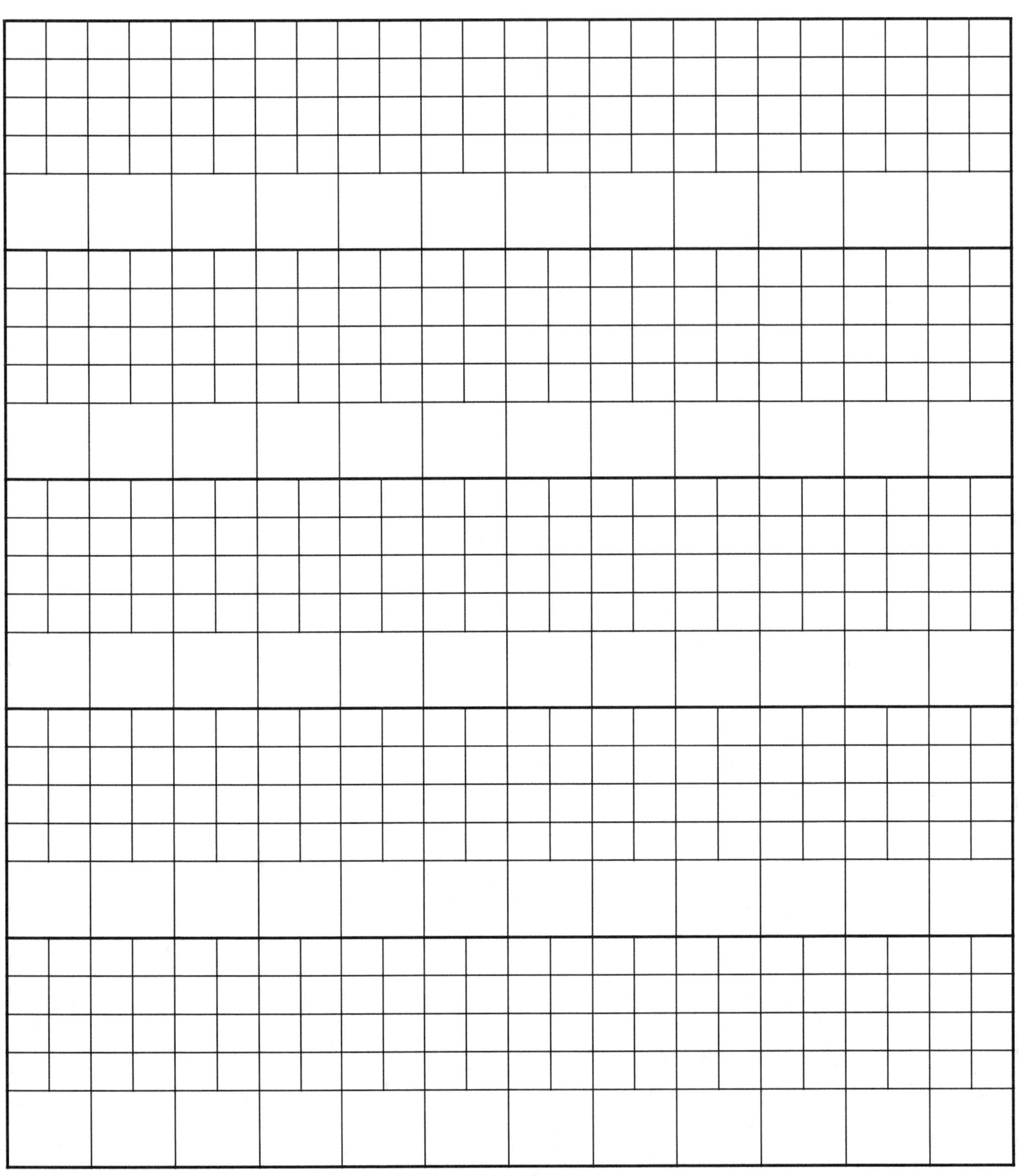

Writing Practice Sheet

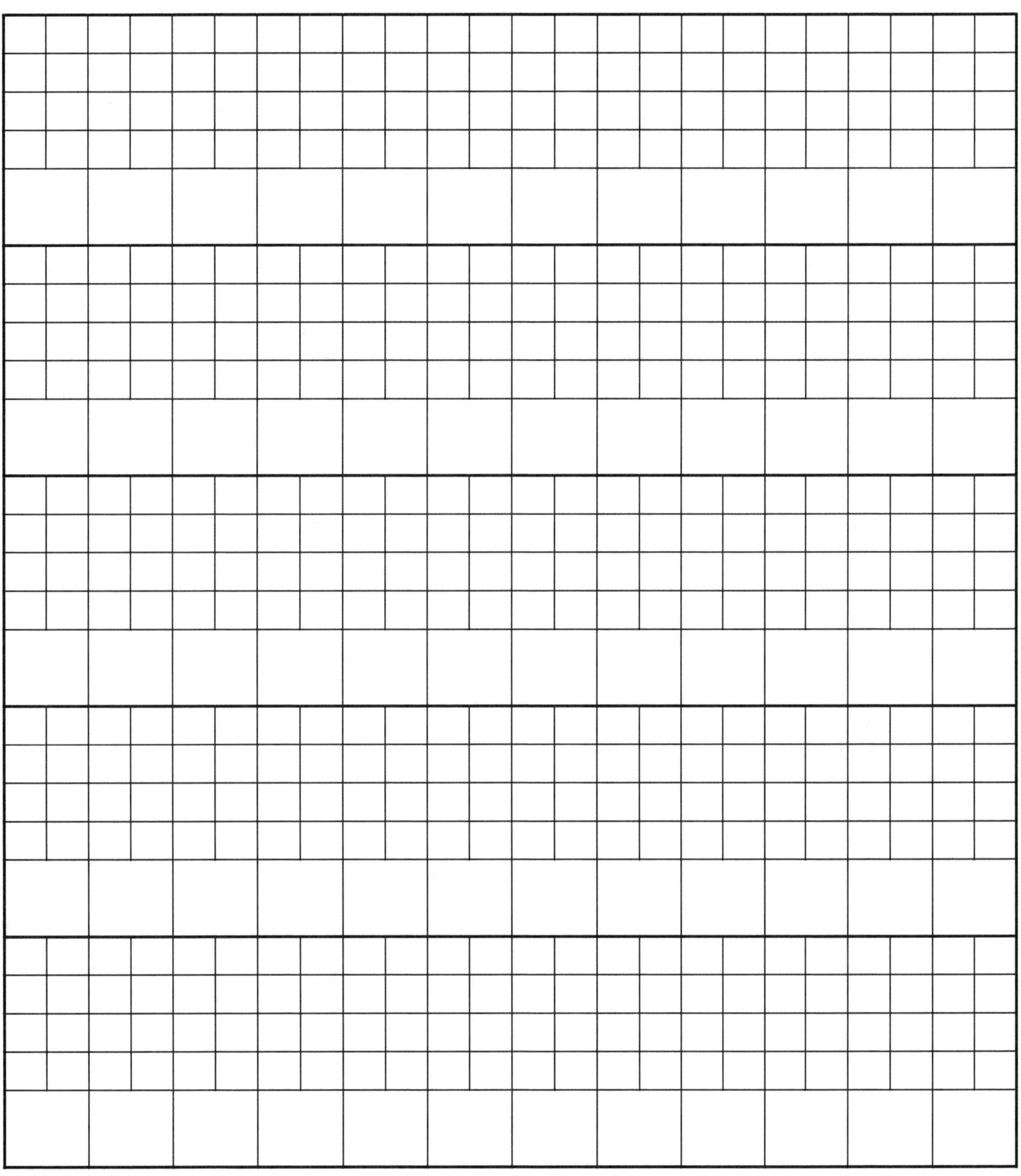

Writing Practice Sheet

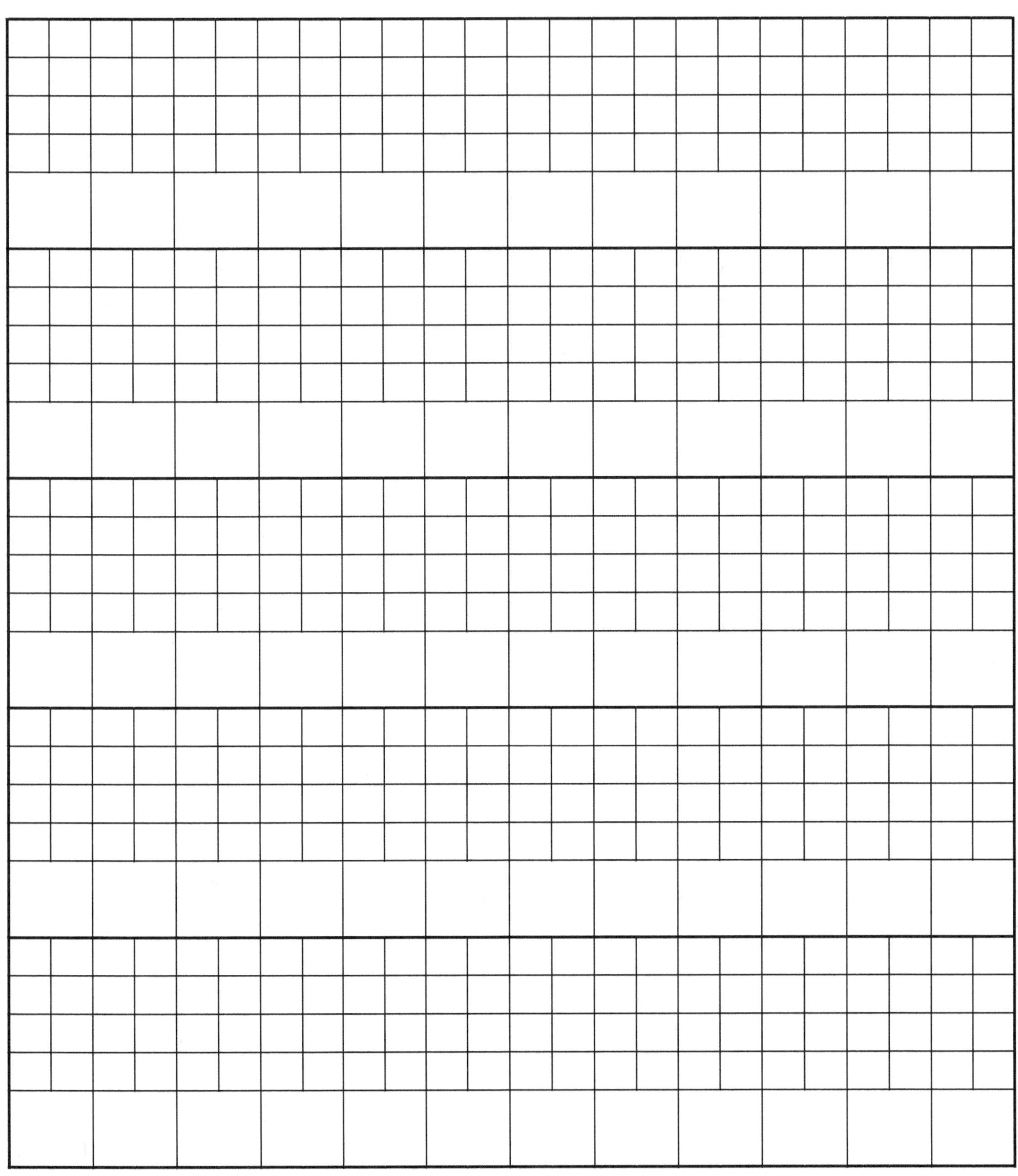

Writing Practice Sheet

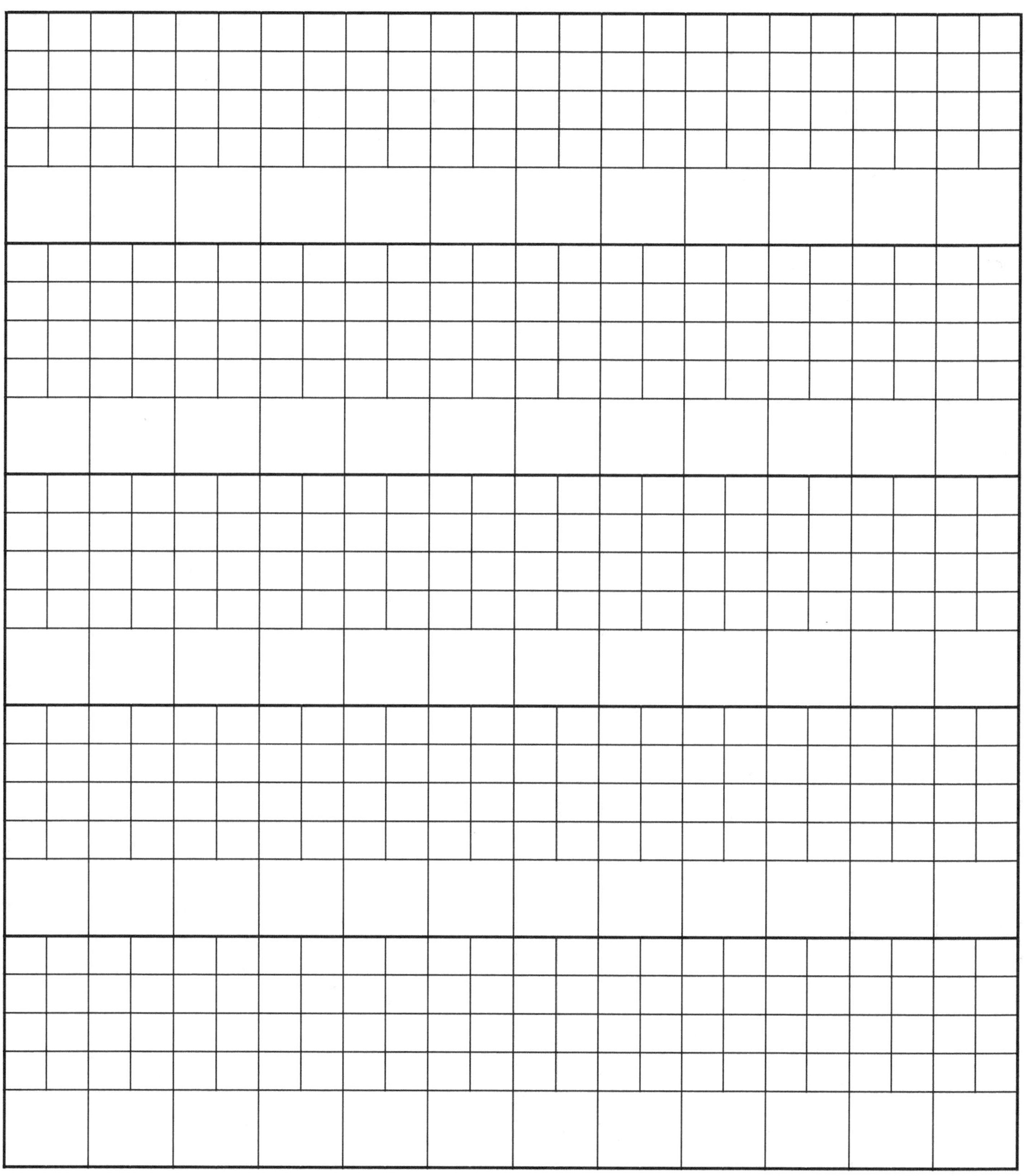

Writing Practice Sheet

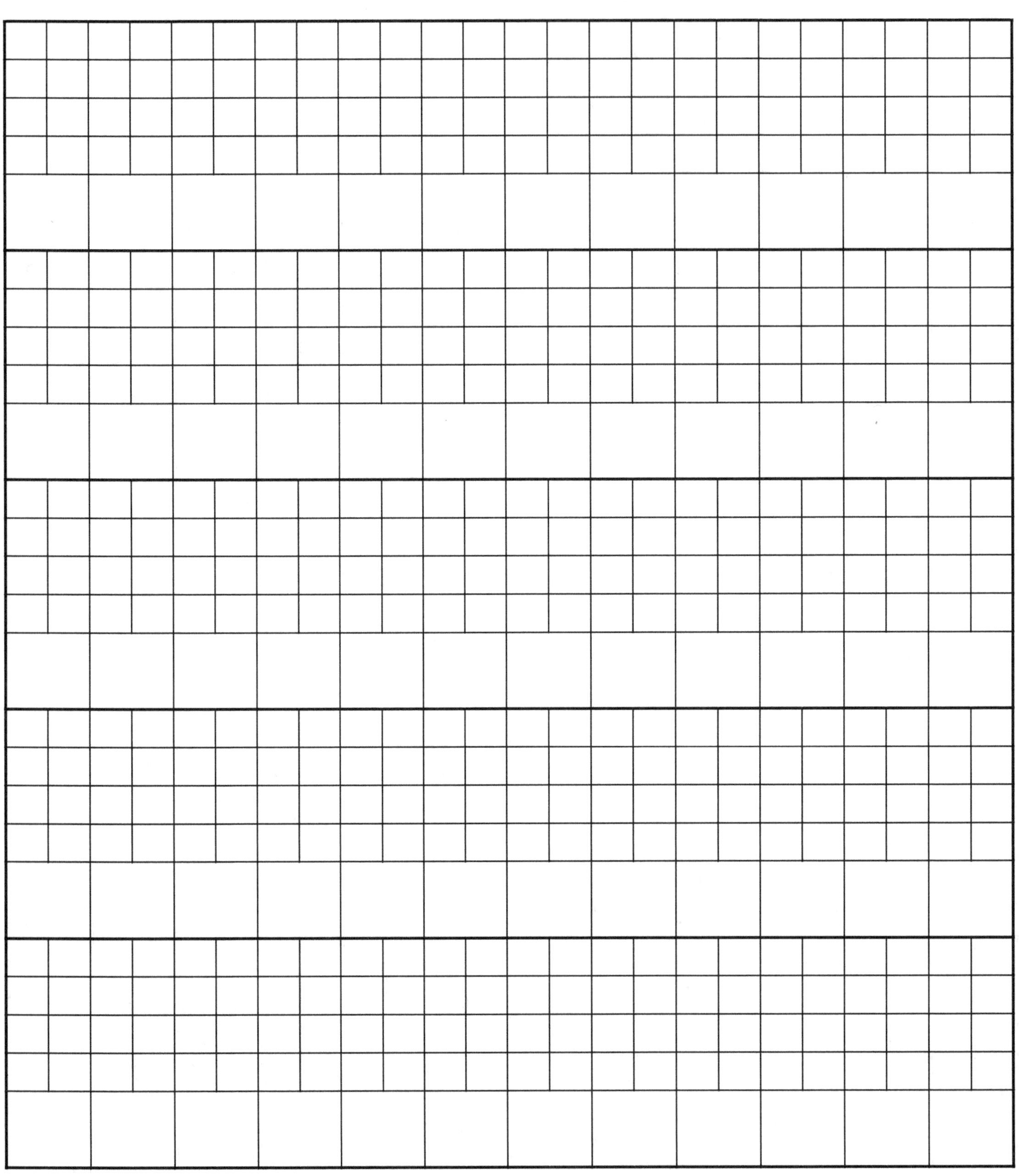

Writing Practice Sheet

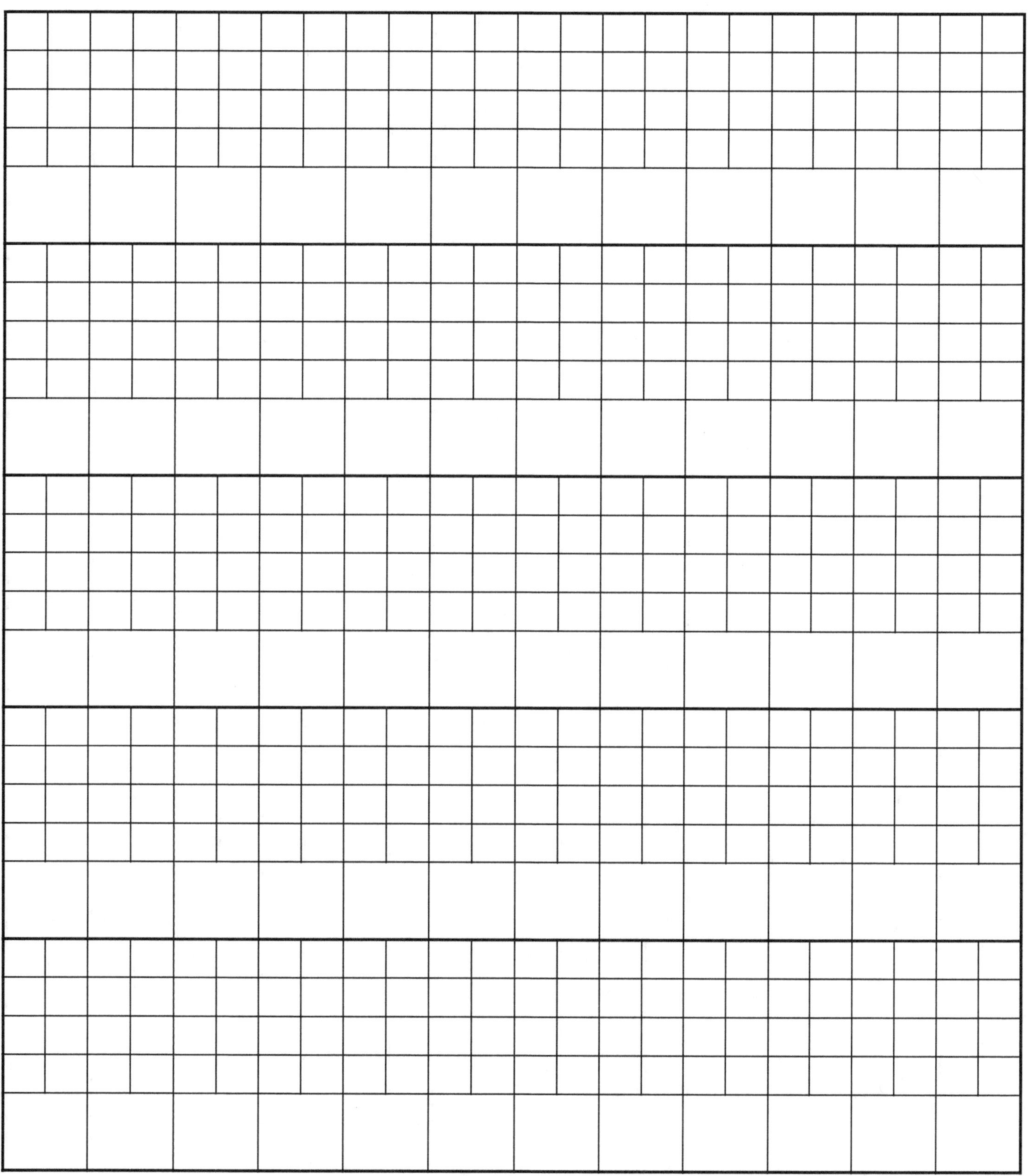

Writing Practice Sheet

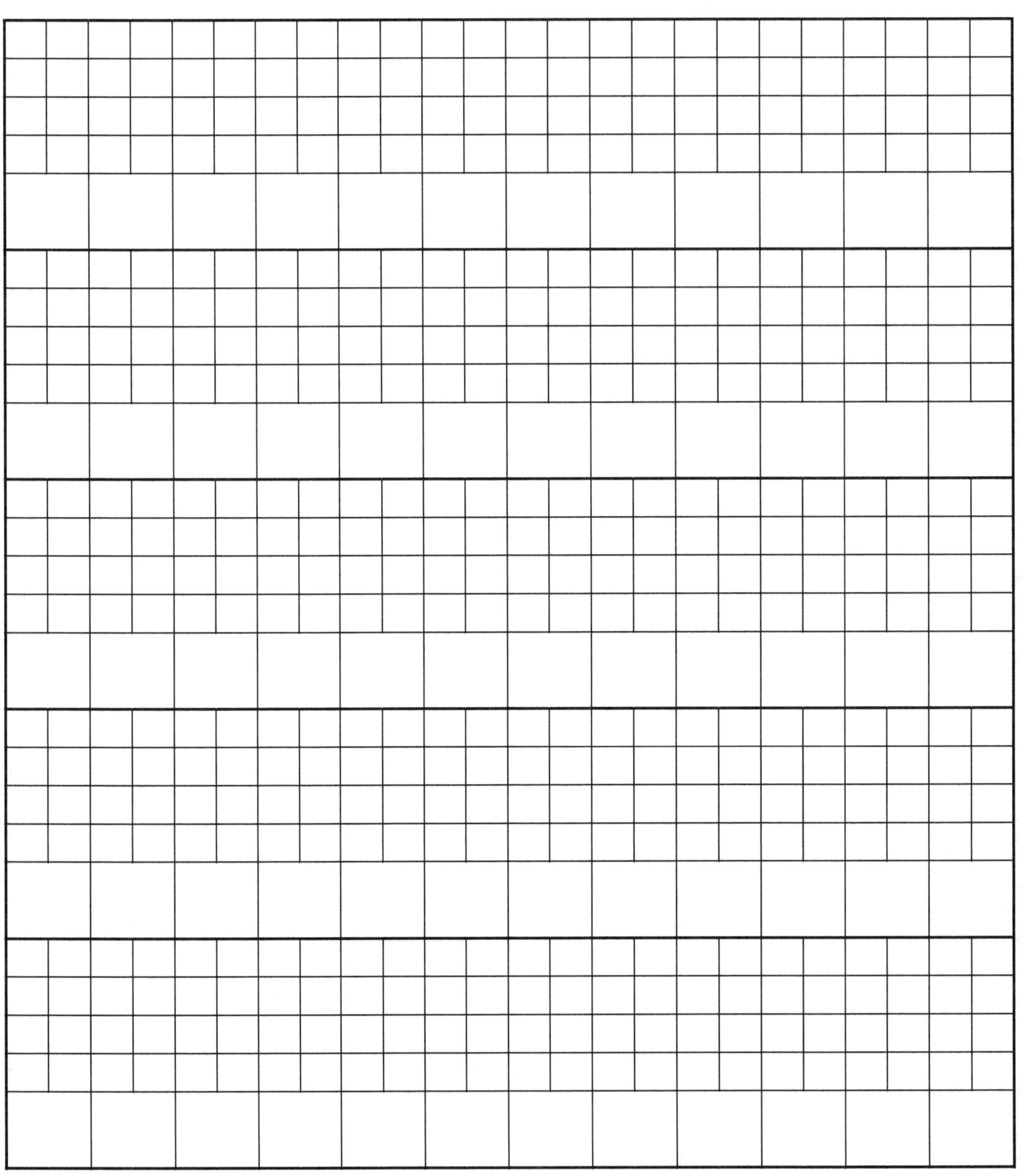

Writing Practice Sheet

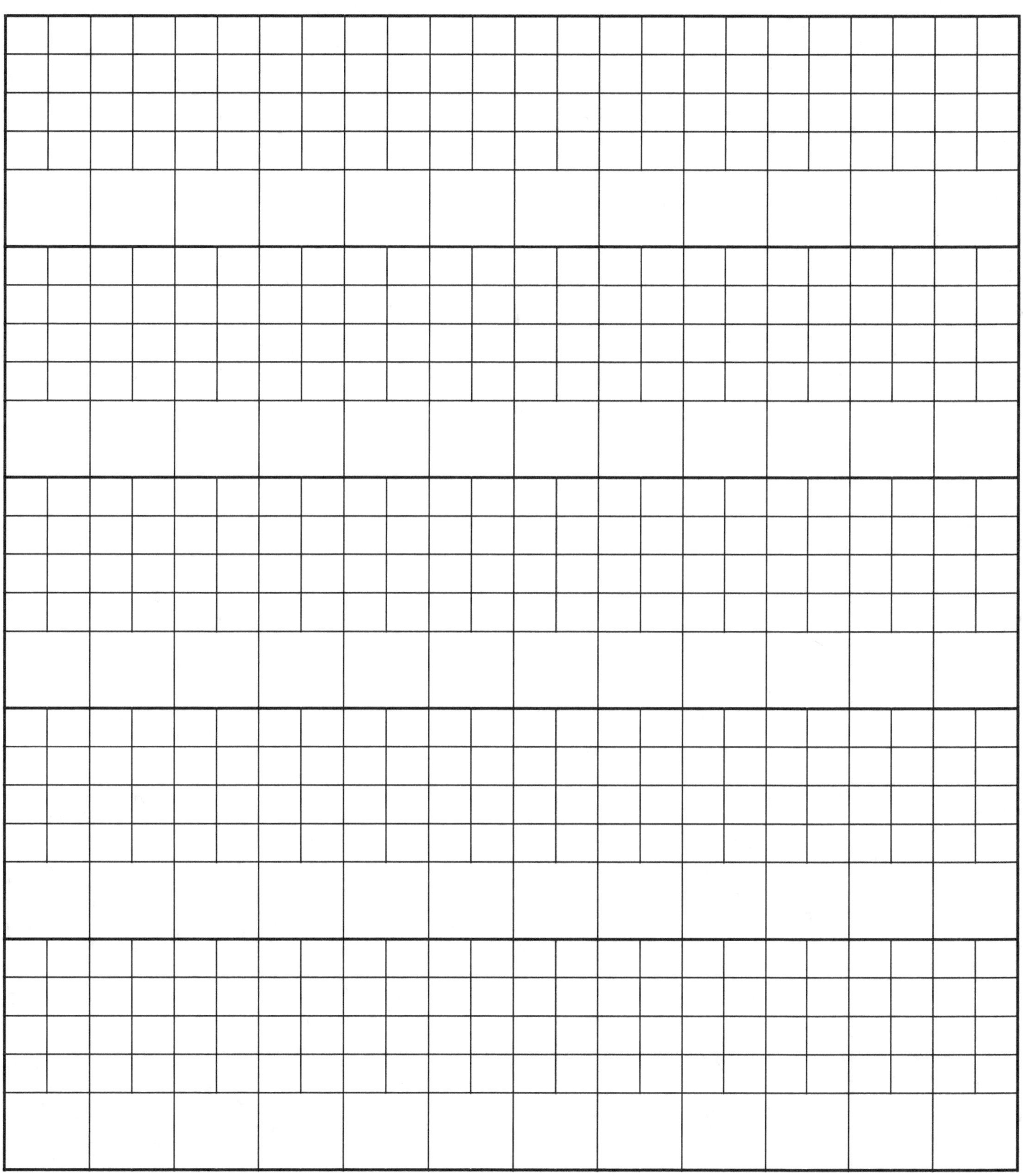

Writing Practice Sheet

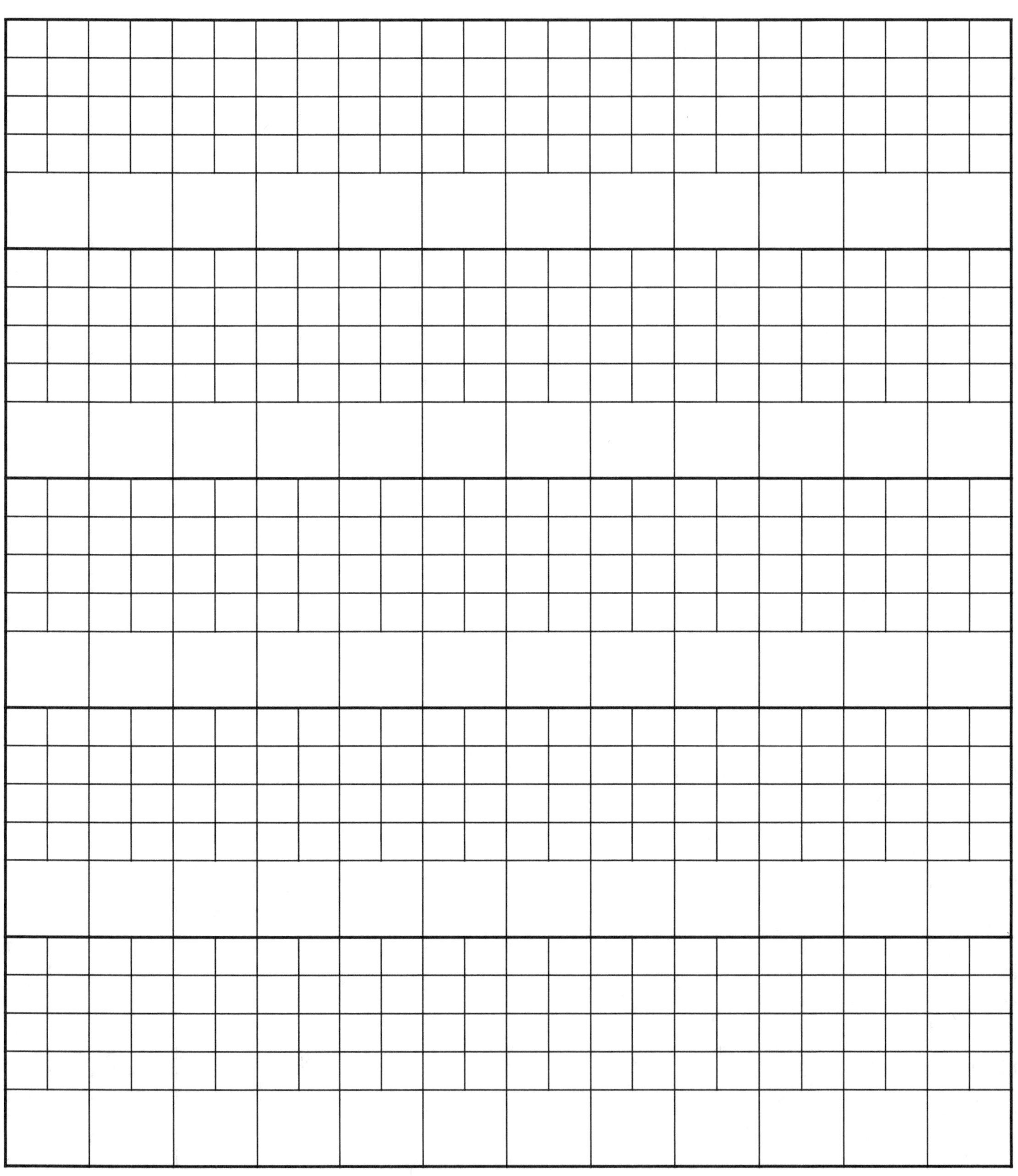

Writing Practice Sheet

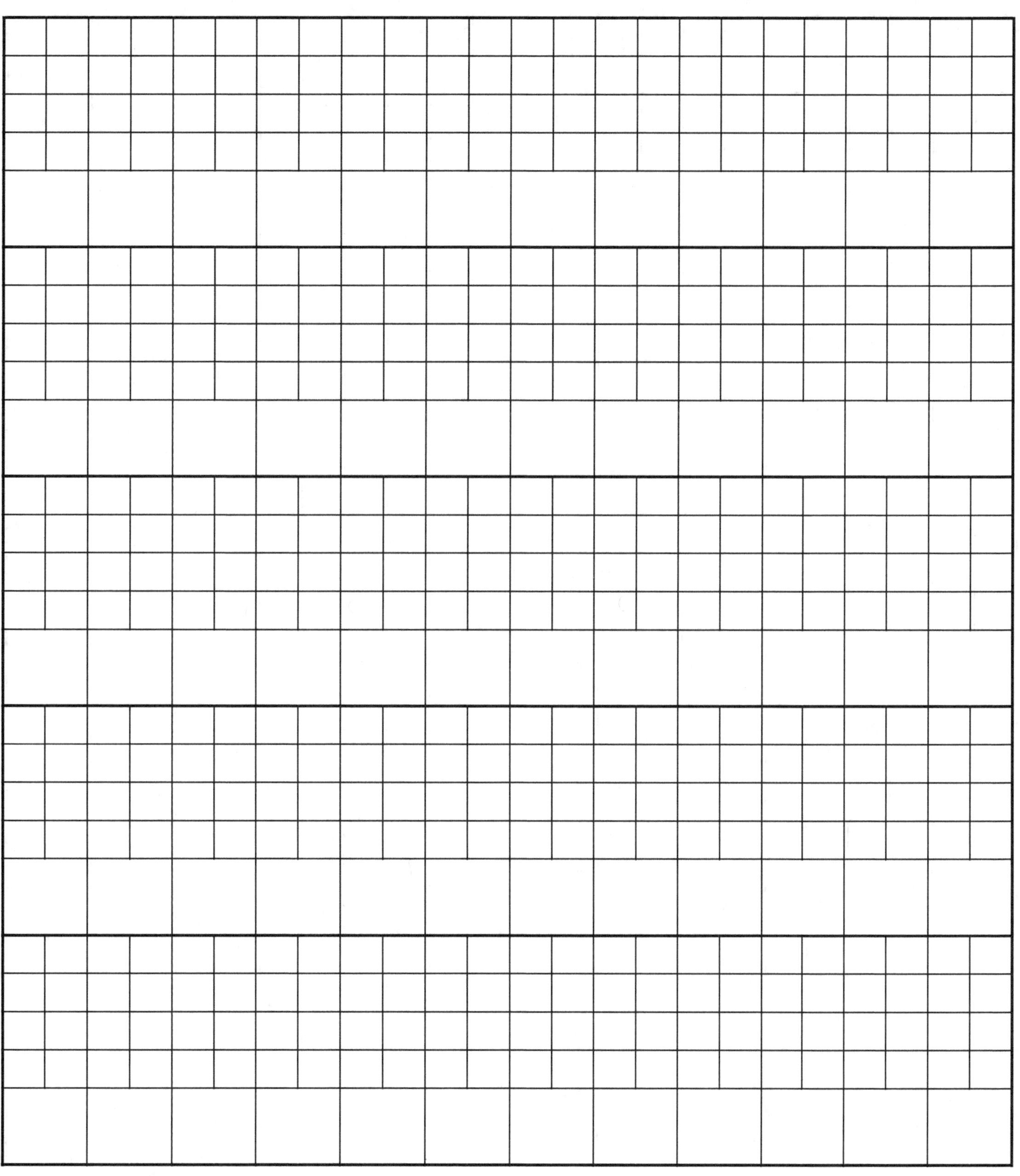

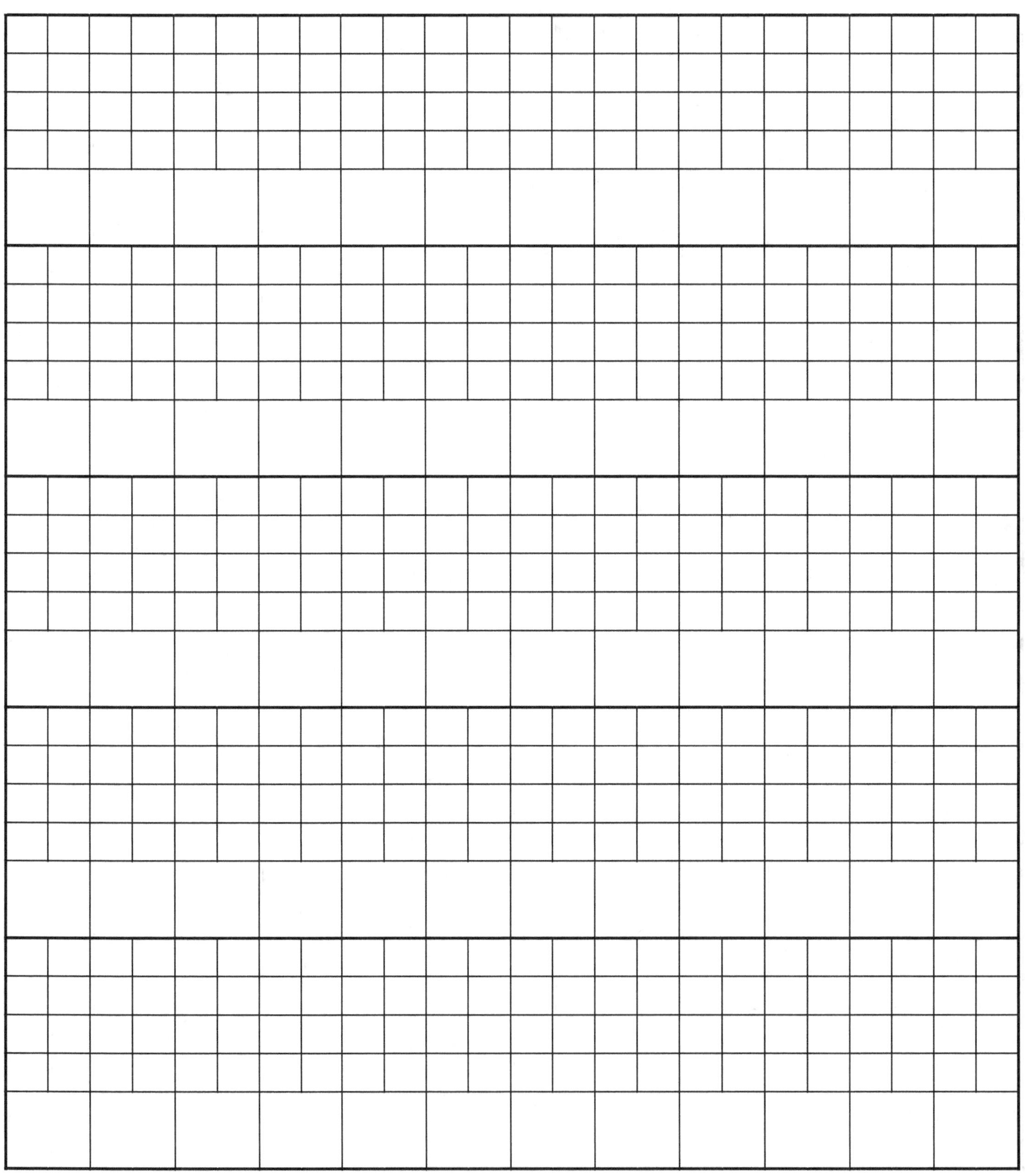

Writing Practice Sheet

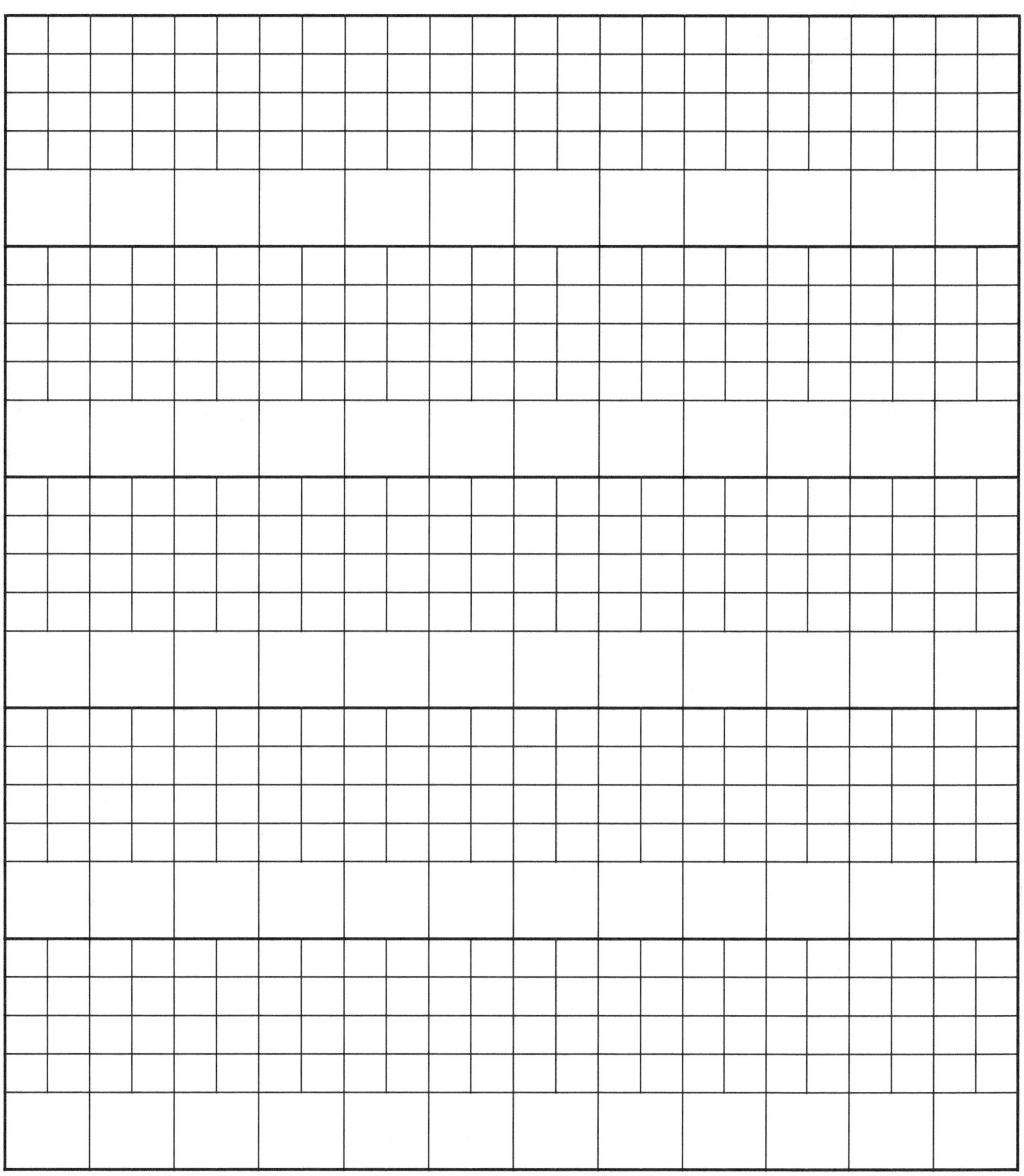

Writing Practice Sheet

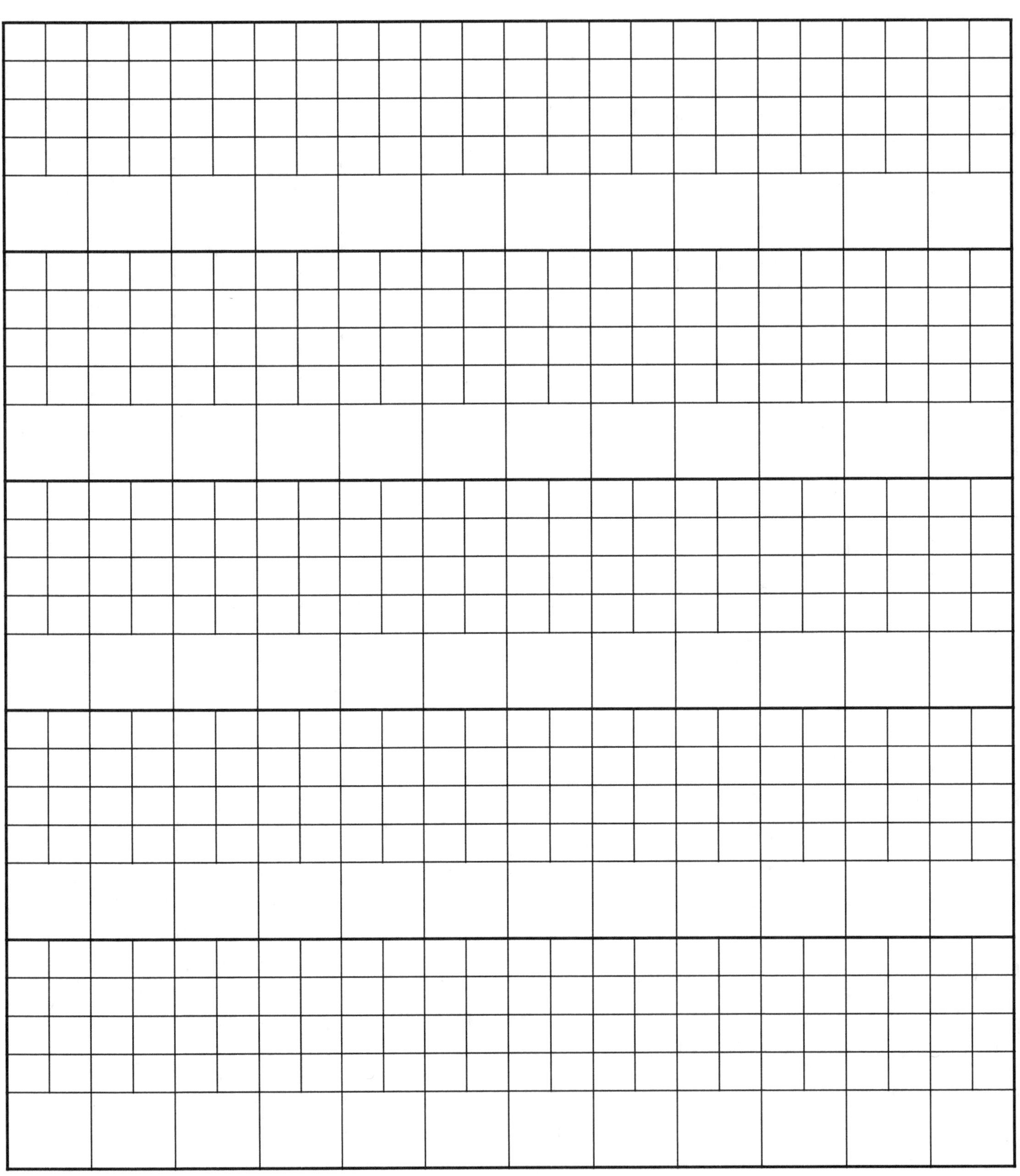

Writing Practice Sheet

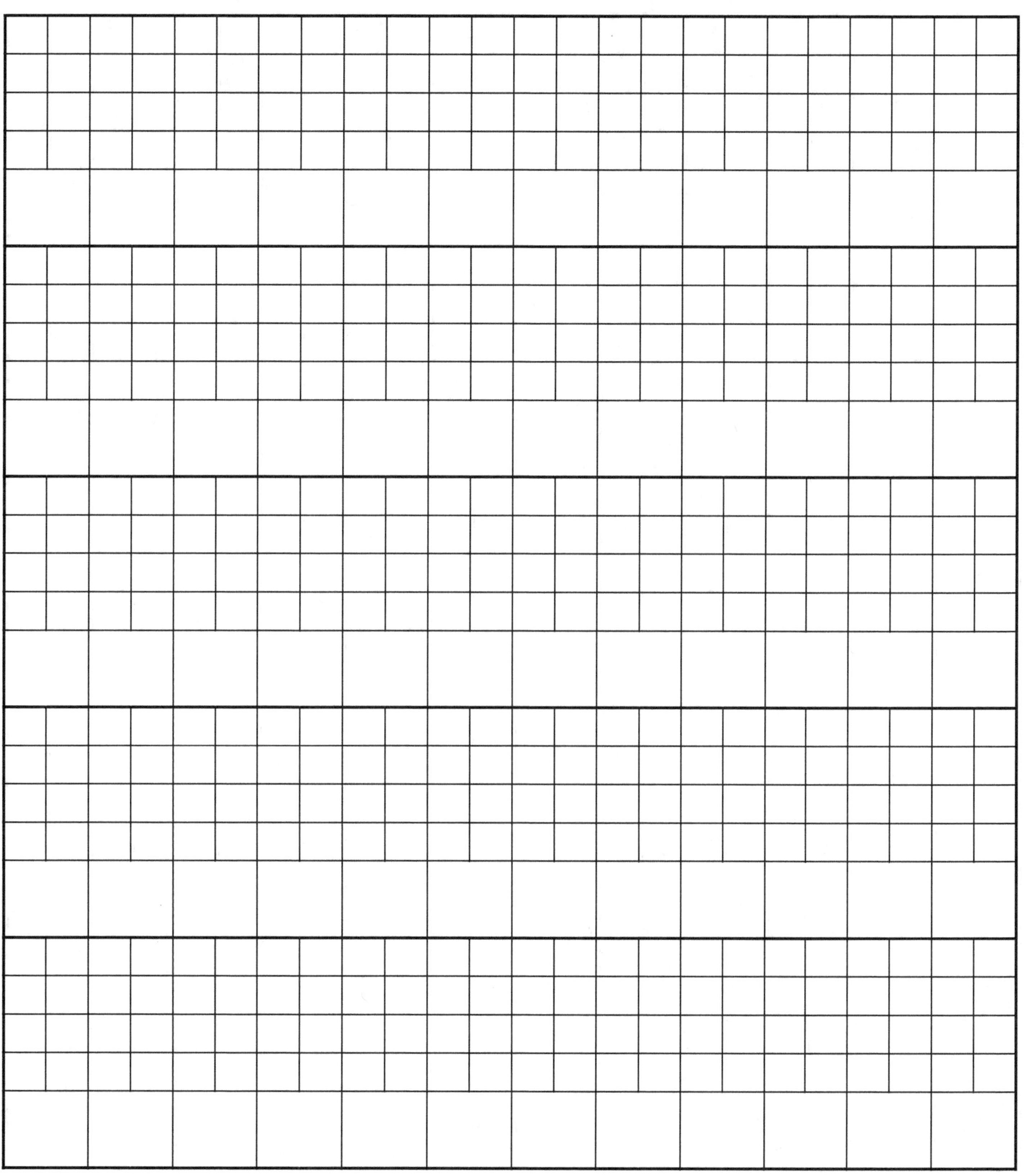

Writing Practice Sheet

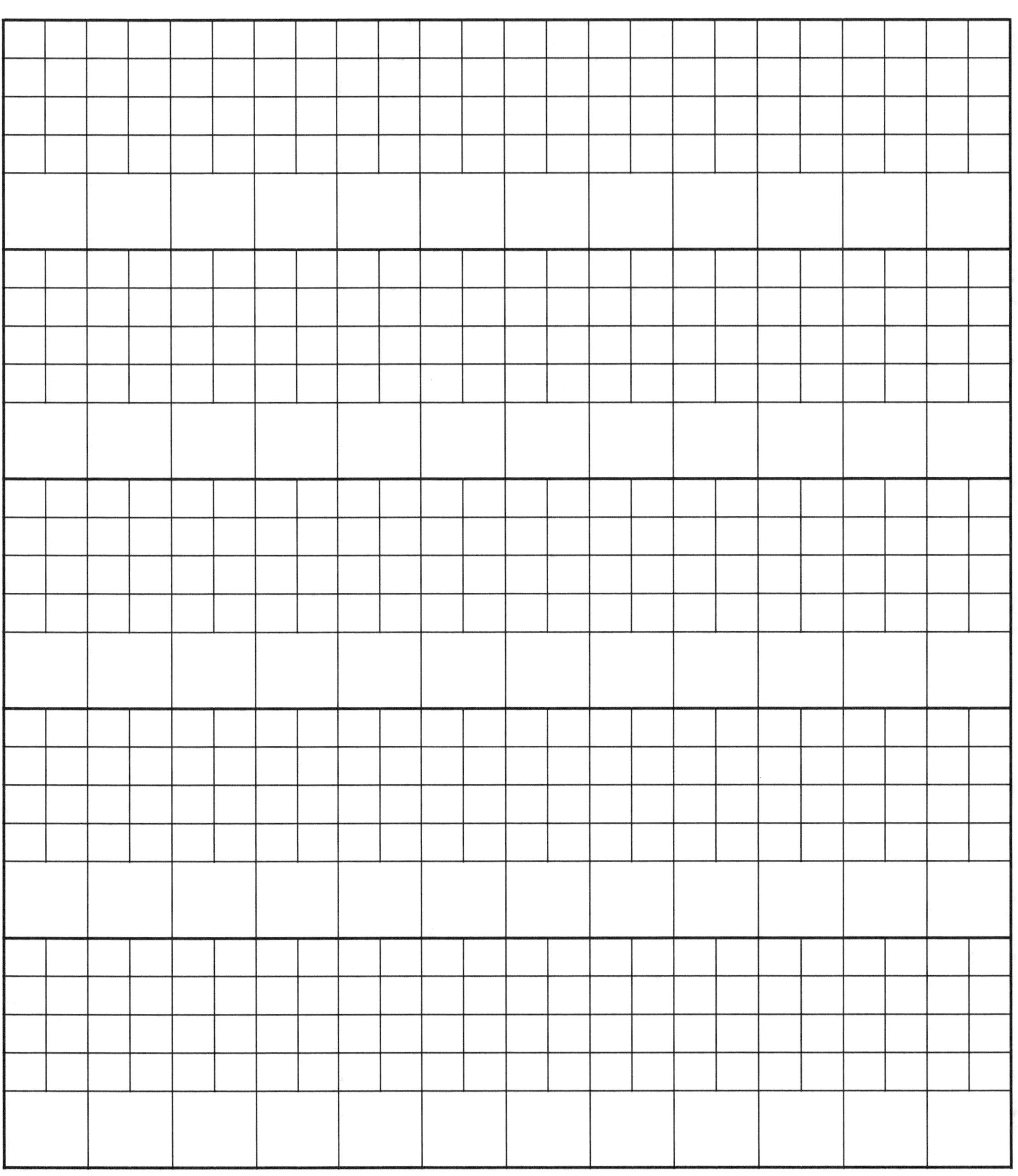

Writing Practice Sheet

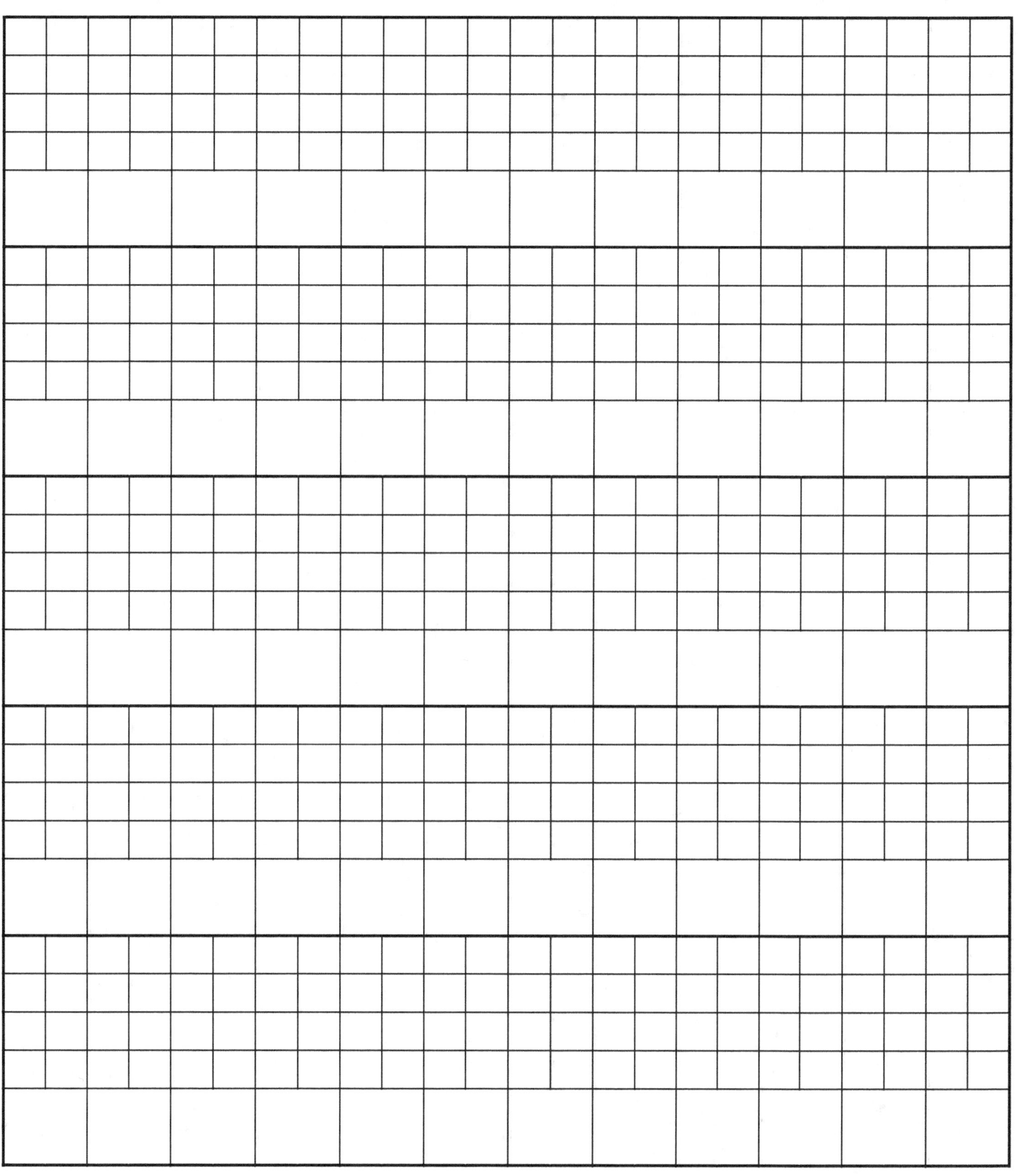

Writing Practice Sheet

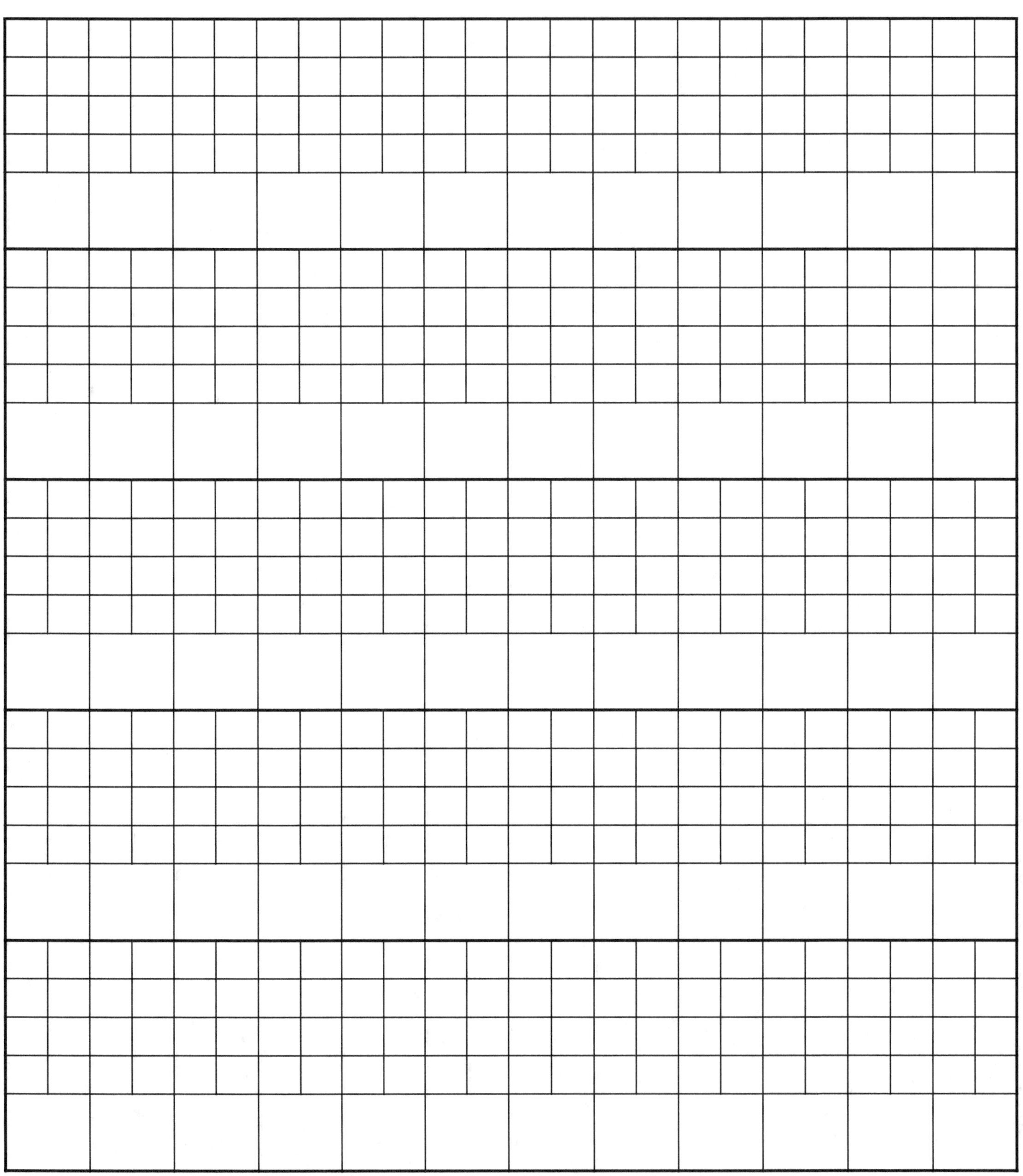

Writing Practice Sheet

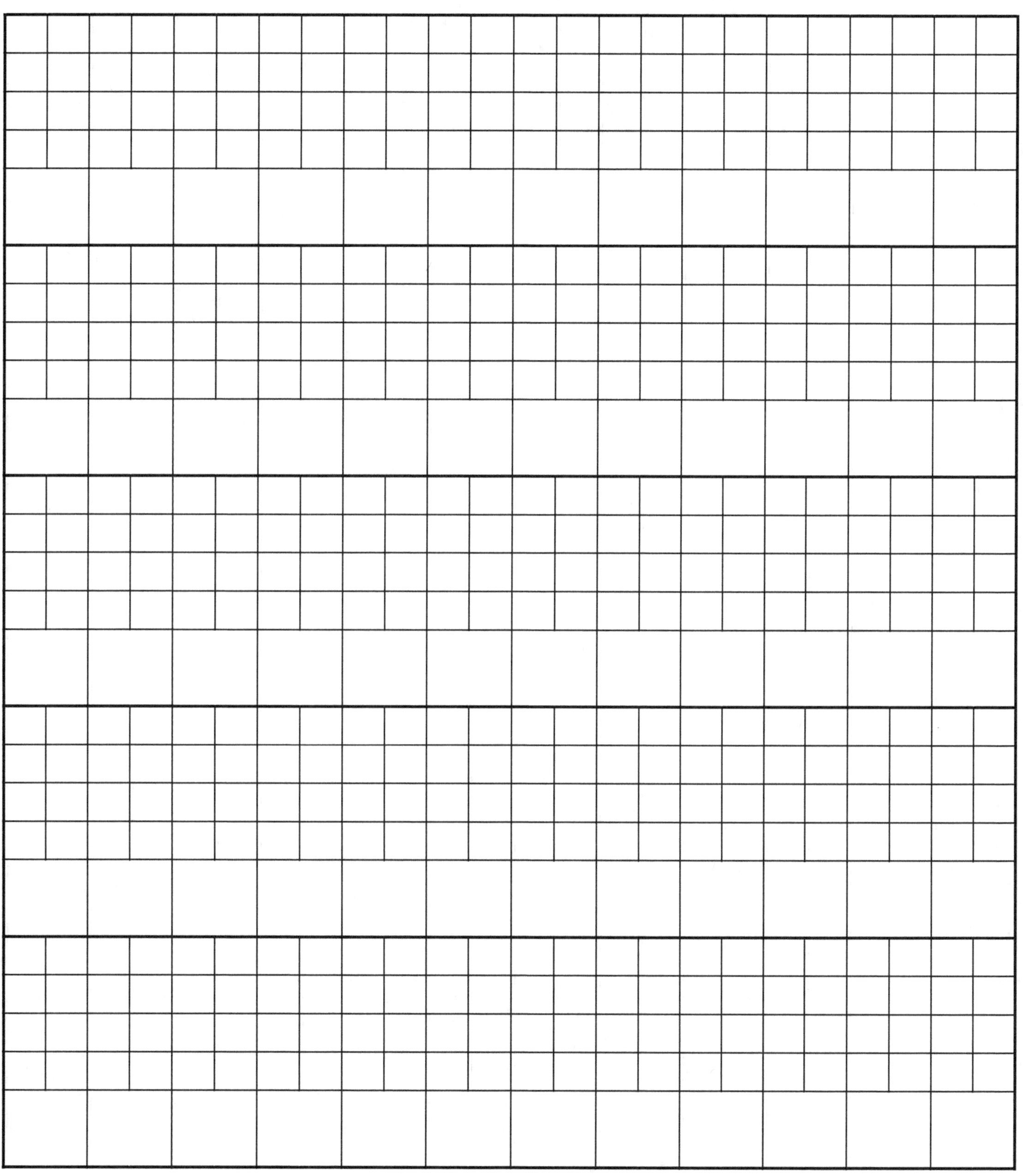

Writing Practice Sheet

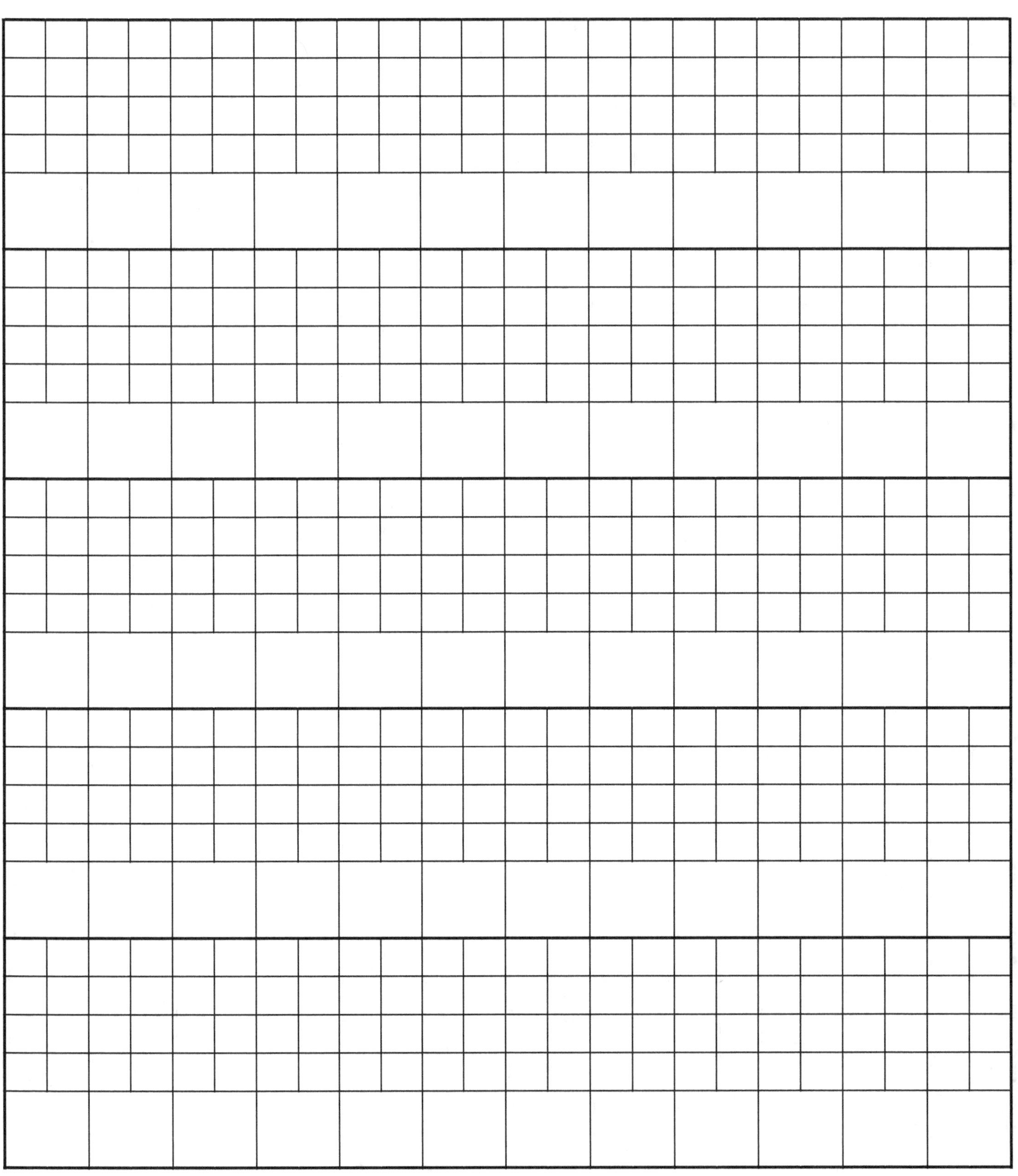

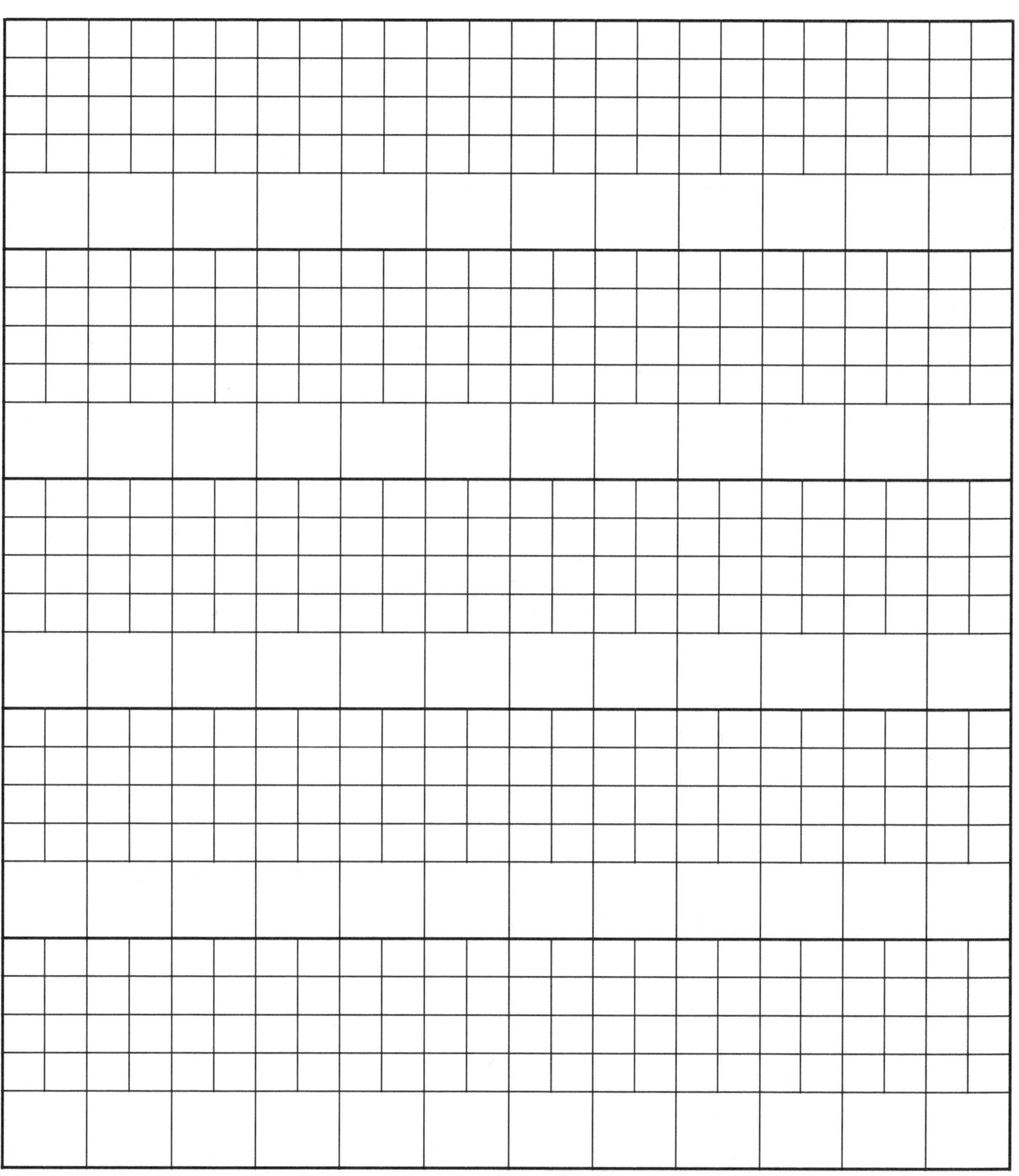

Writing Practice Sheet

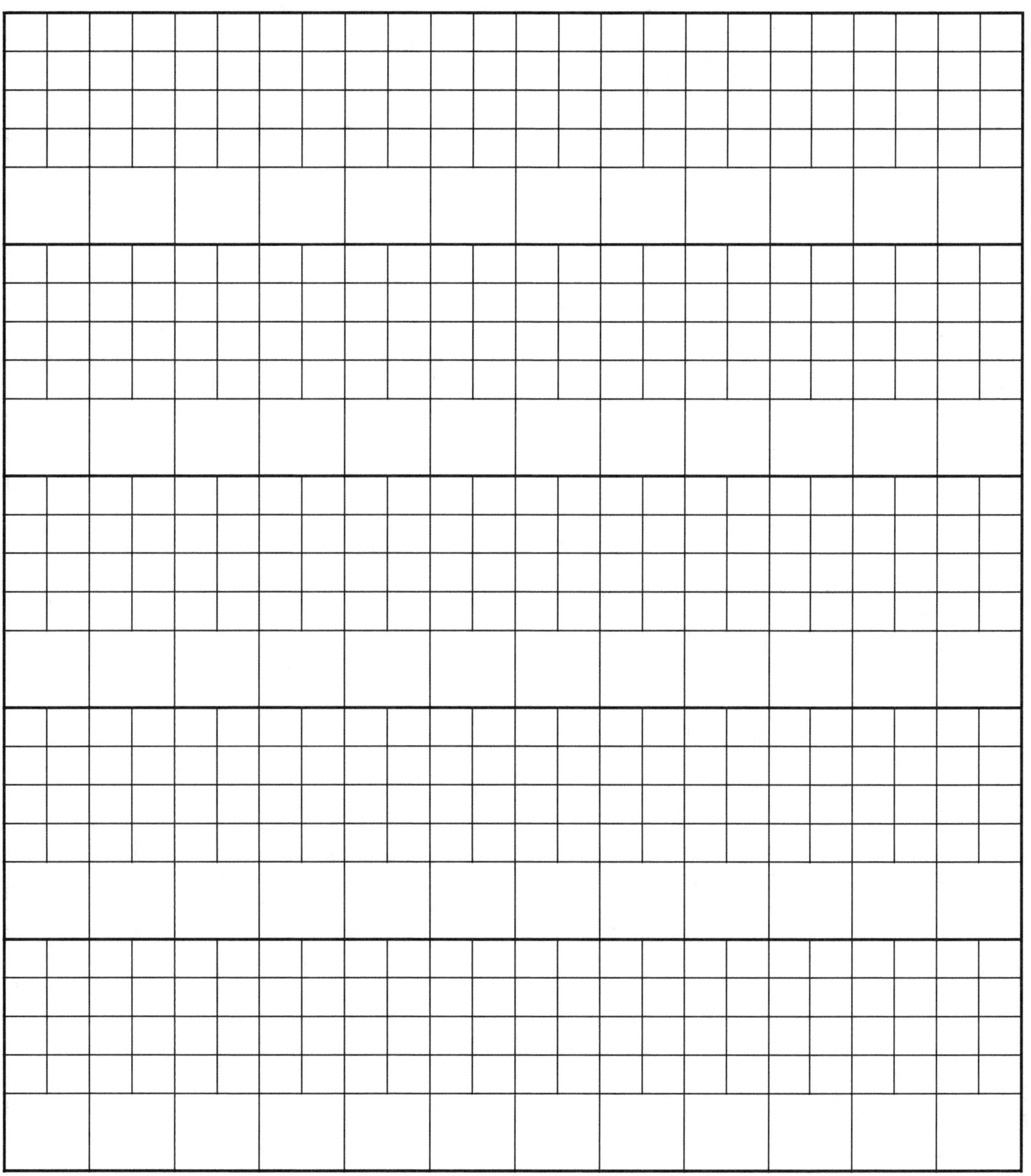

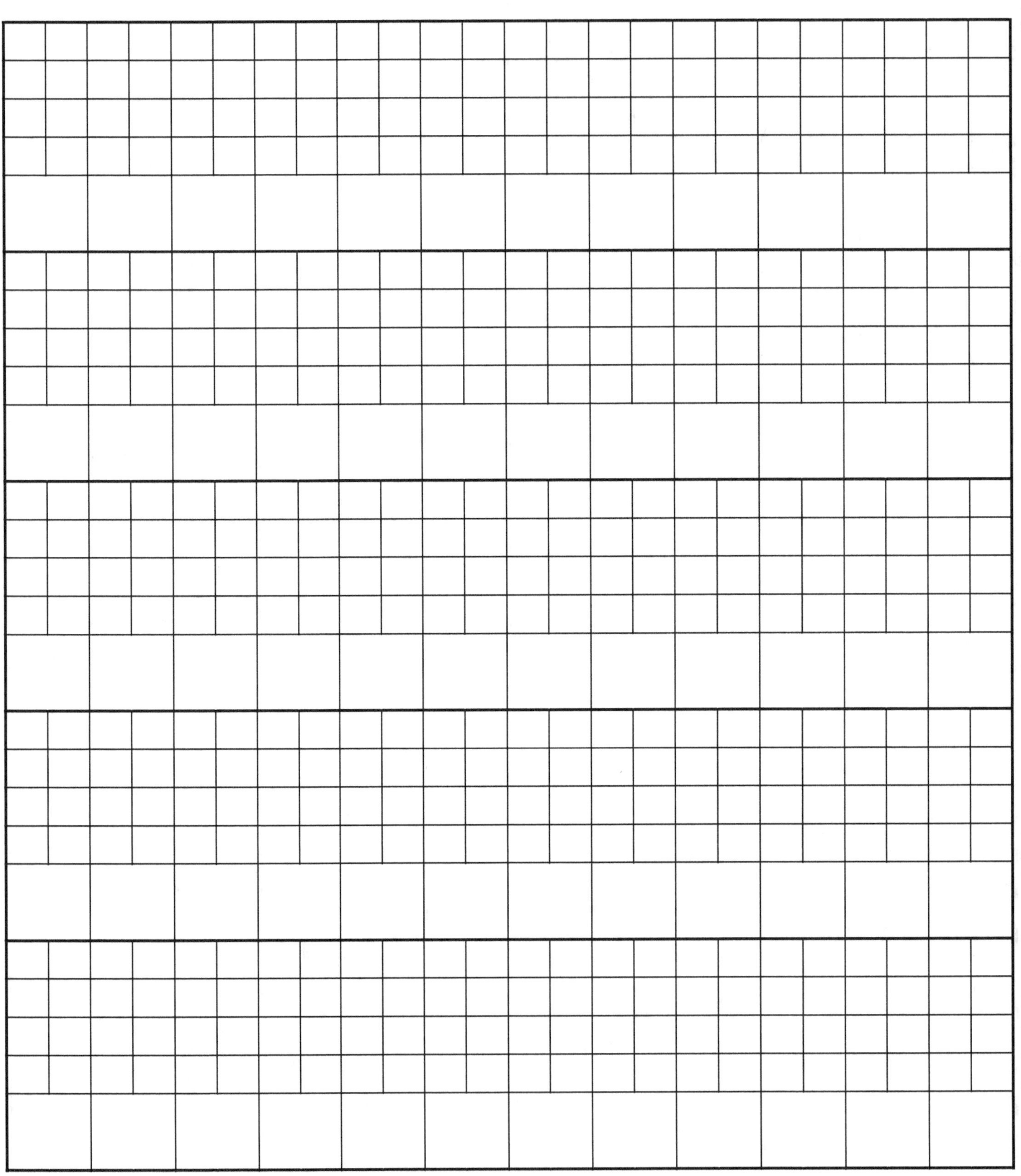

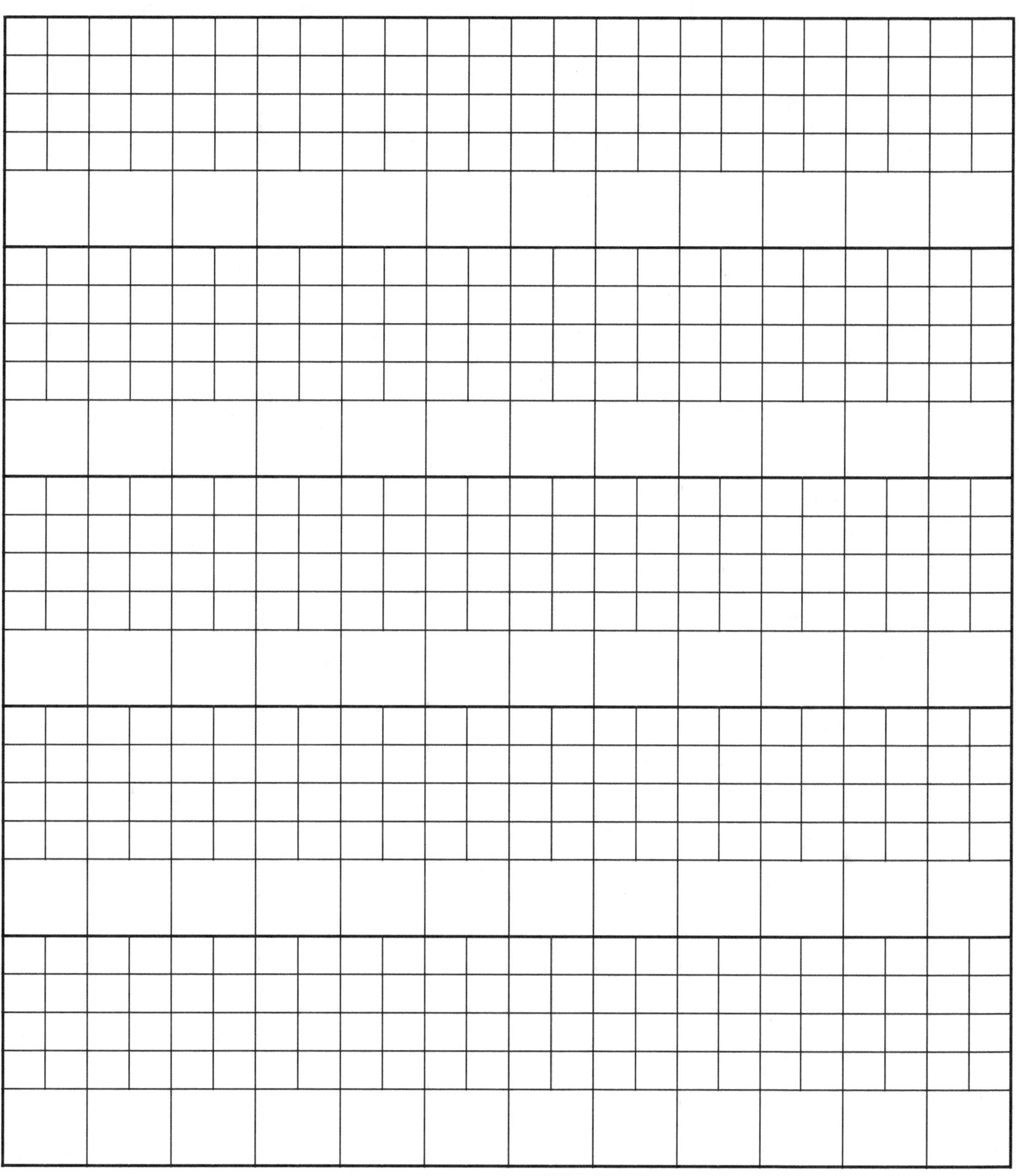

Writing Practice Sheet

Writing Practice Sheet

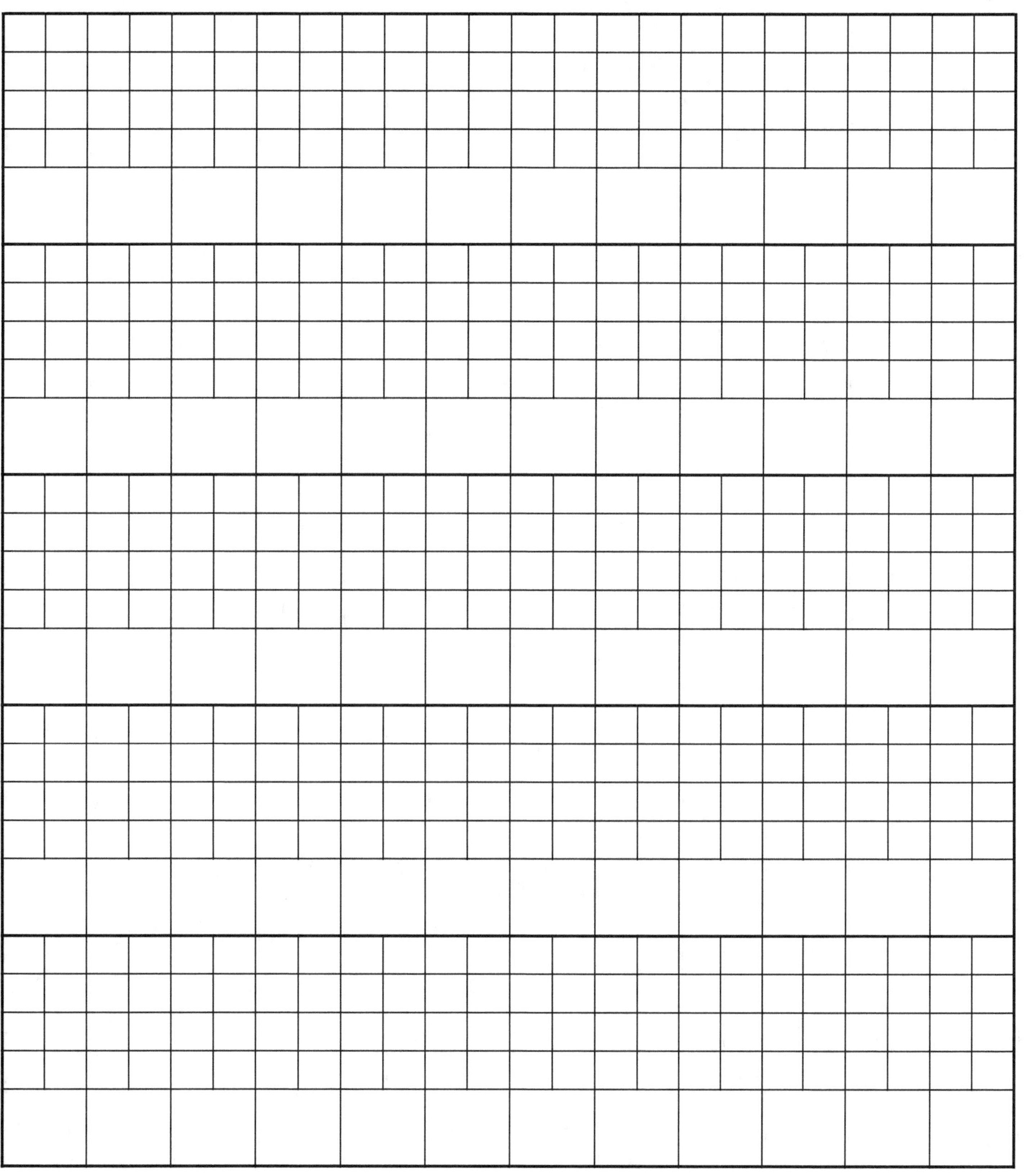

Writing Practice Sheet

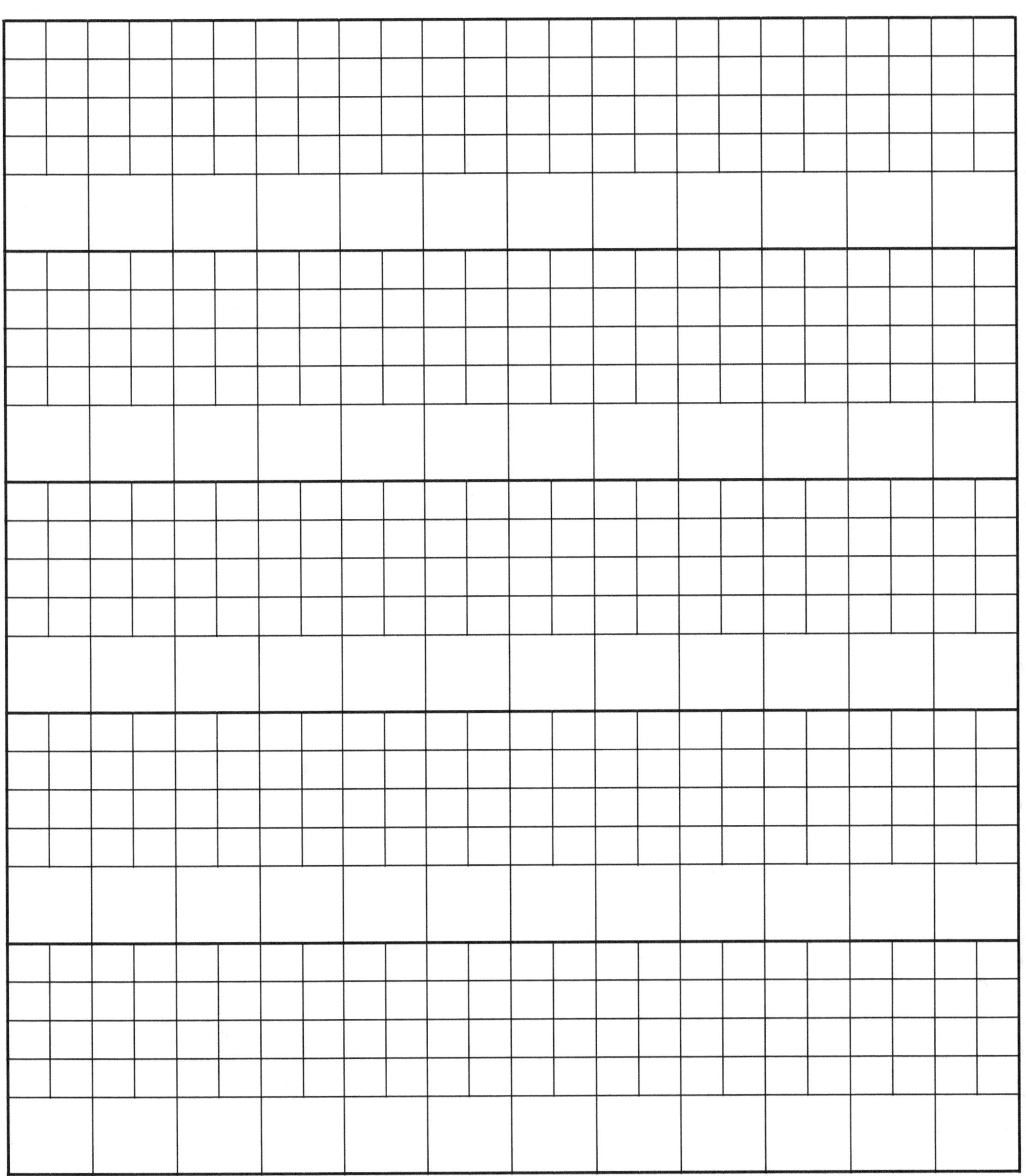

Writing Practice Sheet

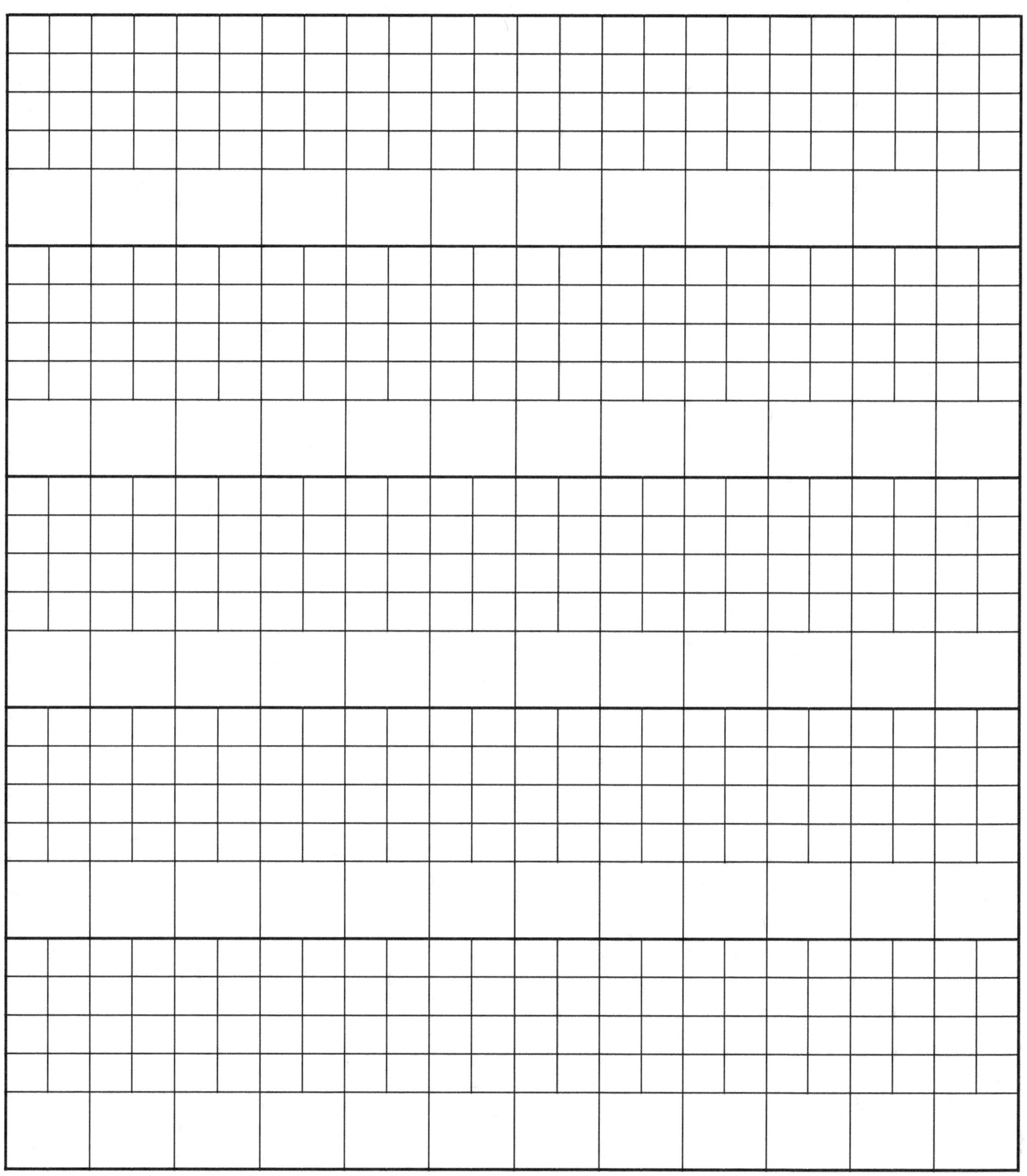

Writing Practice Sheet

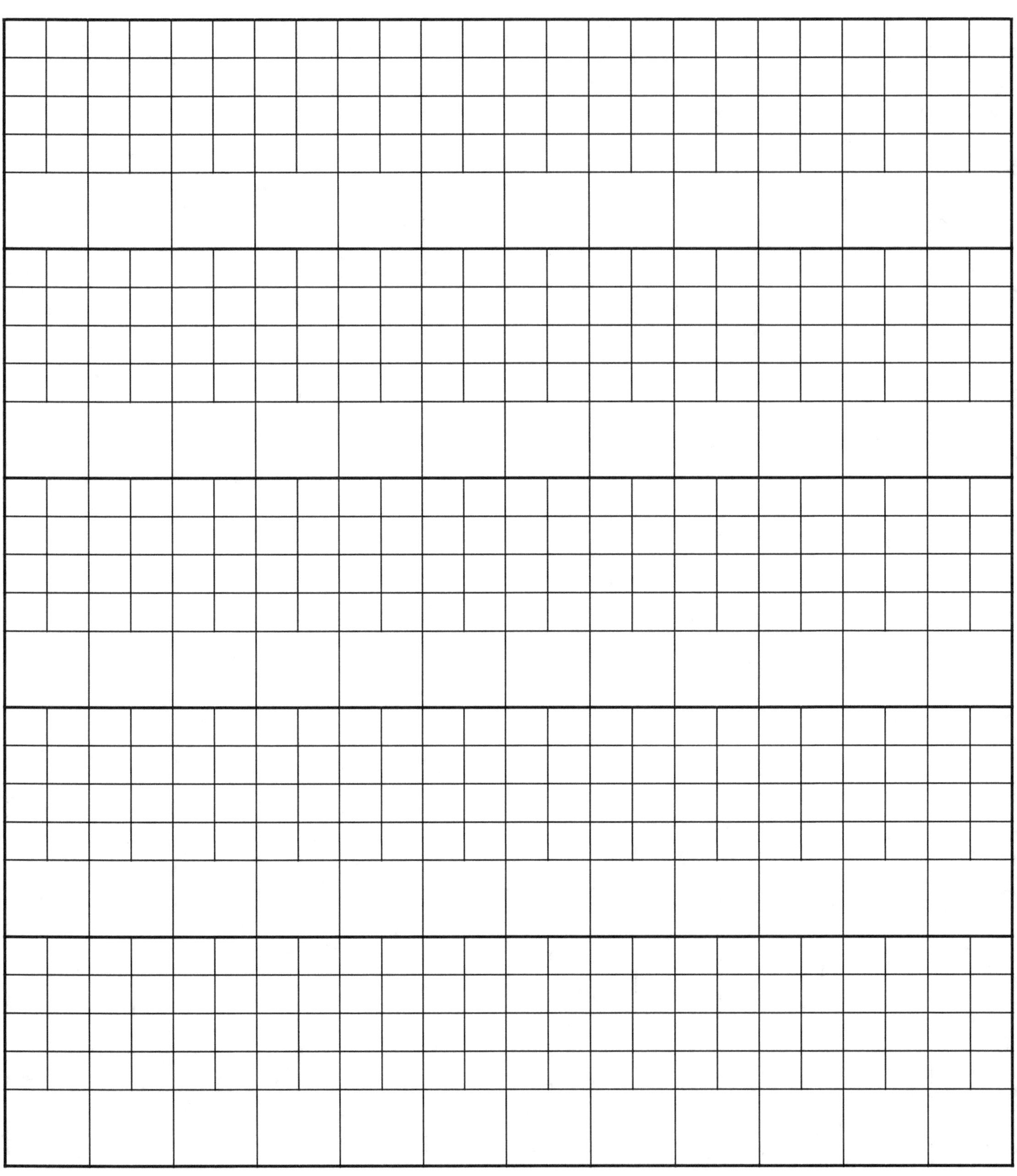

Writing Practice Sheet

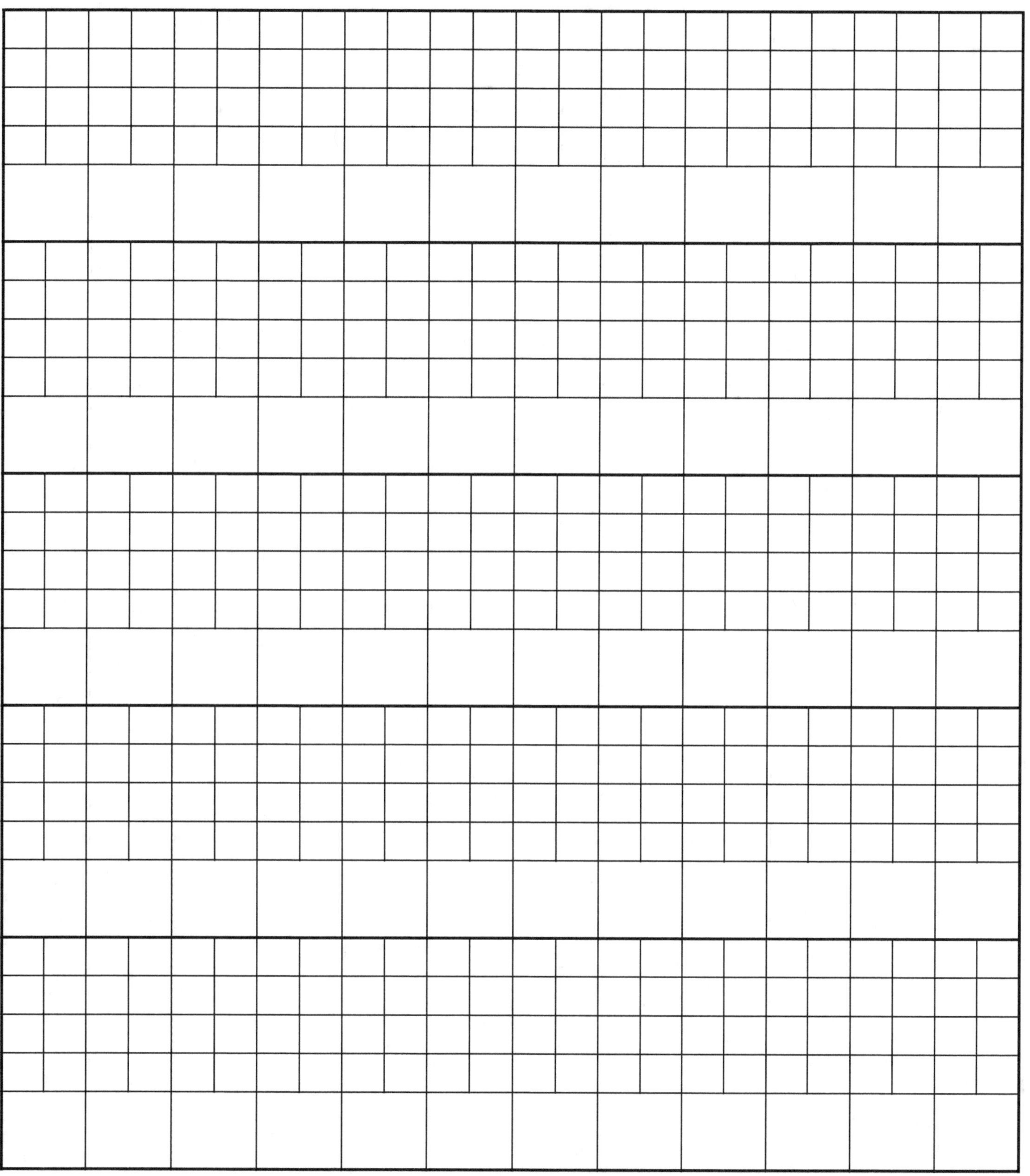

Writing Practice Sheet

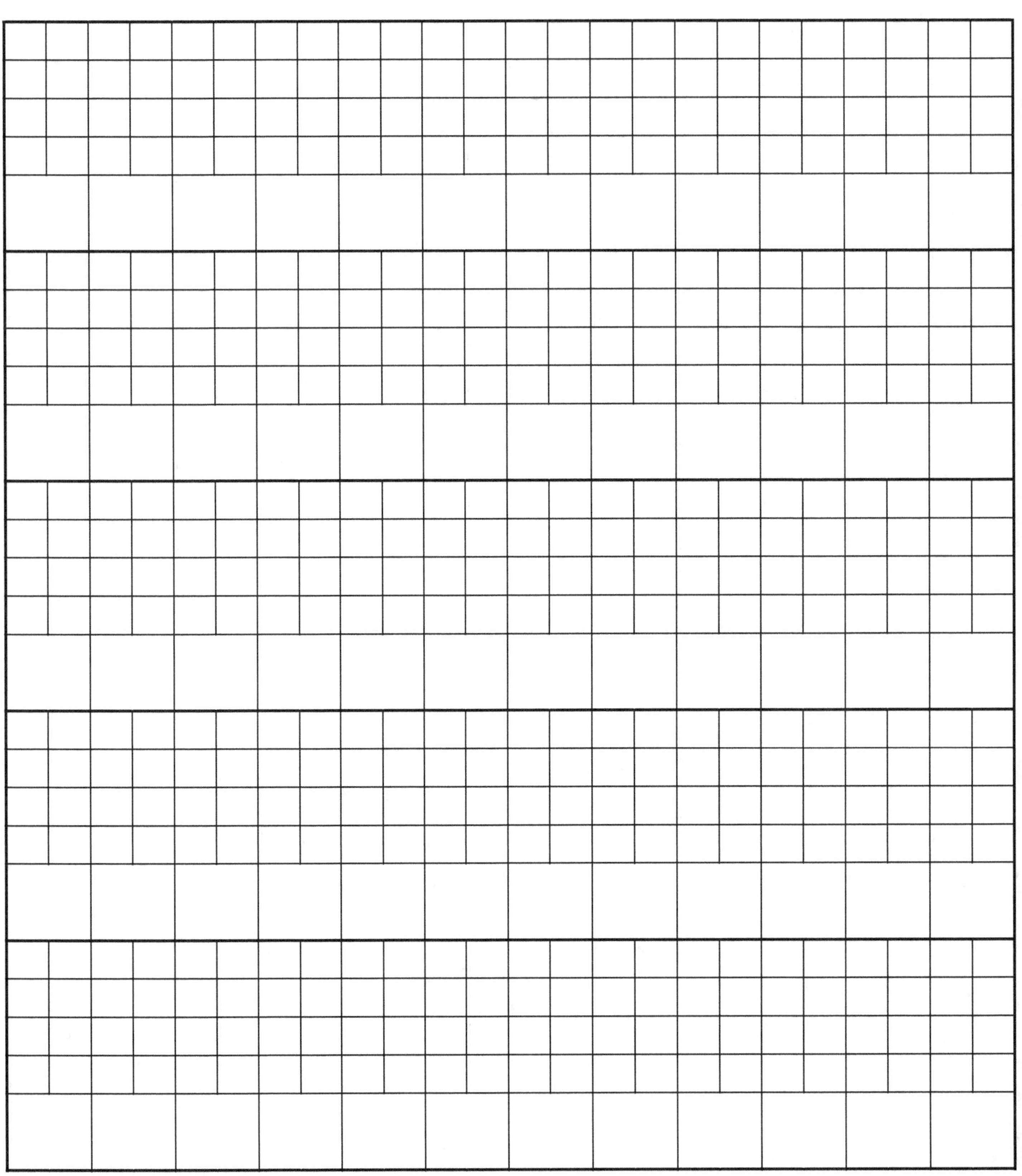

Writing Practice Sheet

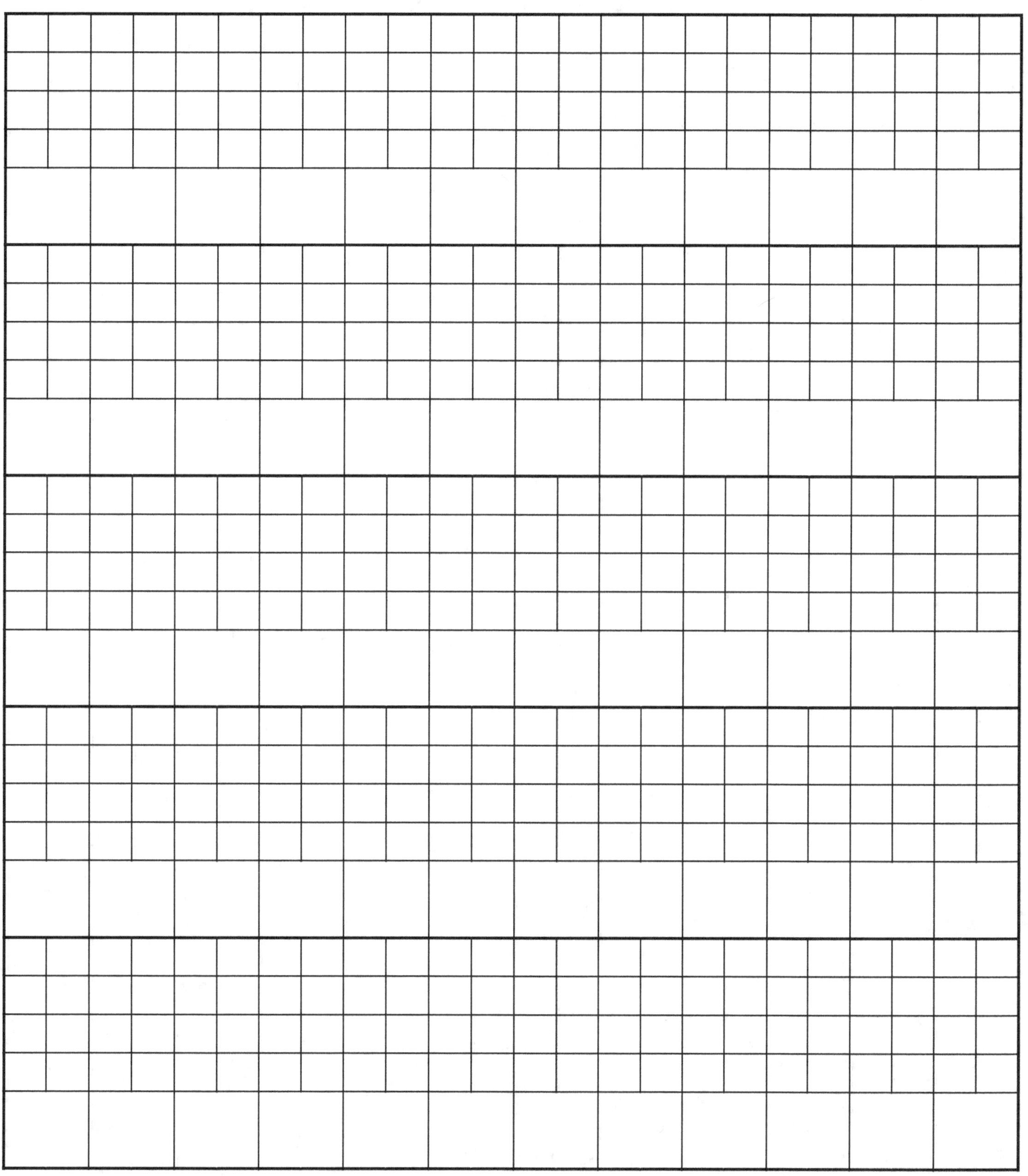

Writing Practice Sheet

Writing Practice Sheet

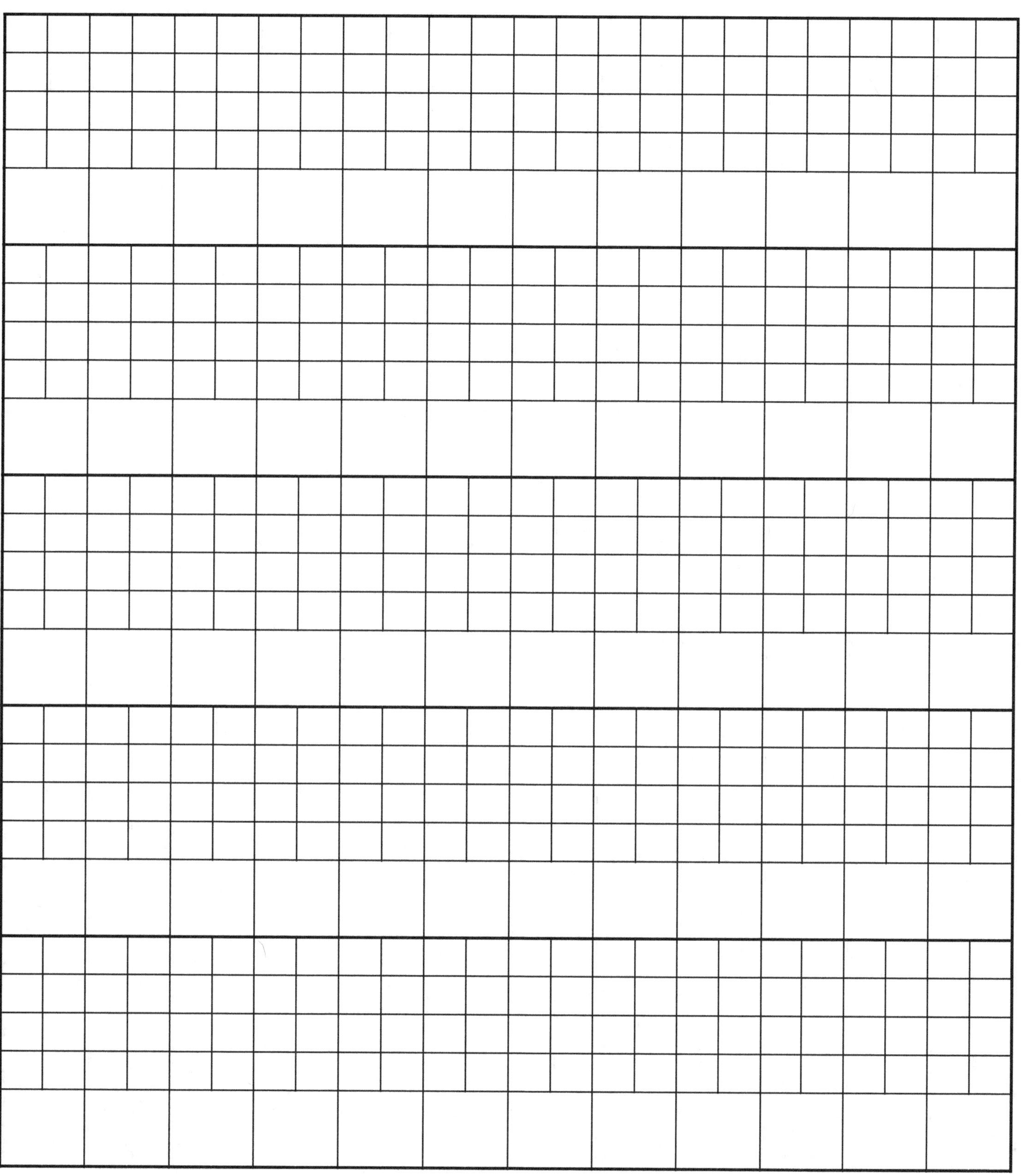

Writing Practice Sheet

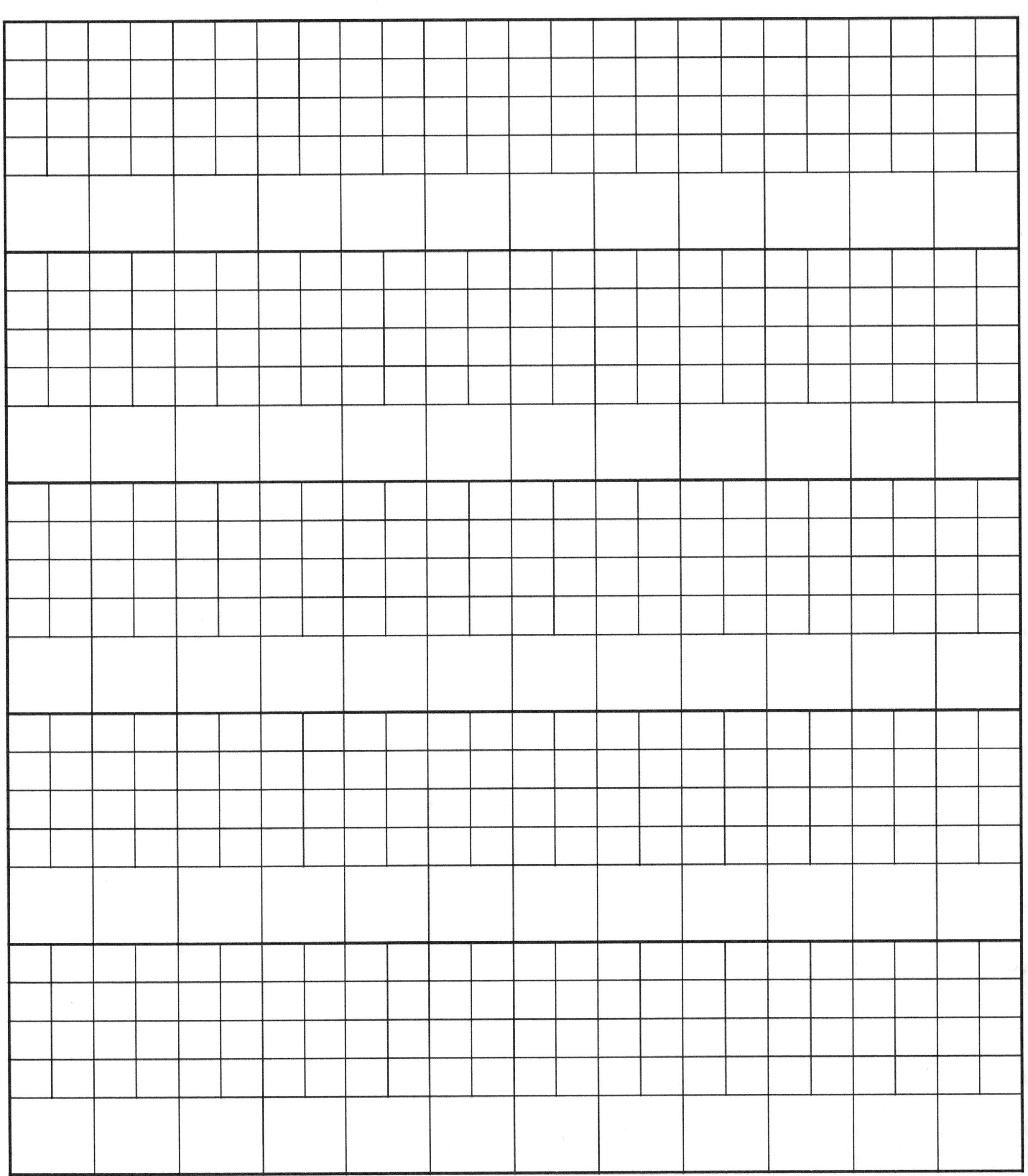